PATHWAYS TO JOY

PATHWAYS TO JOY

Eileen Mitson

Eagle Publishing, Atworth, Bath, UK

This edition, © 2007 by Eileen Mitson.
Published 2007 by Eagle Publishing Ltd, Unit 2, Bath Road,
Atworth Business Park, Atworth, Wiltshire, SN12 8SB.

The right of Eileen Mitson to be identified as the Author of the Work has been
asserted by her in accordance with the Copyright, Design and Patents Act 1988.

British Library Cataloguing in Publication Data. A catalogue record for this book
is available from the British Library.

Typeset by Eagle Publishing Ltd
Printed by Creative Print and Design, Wales
ISBN: 978 0 86347 6310

TABLE OF CONTENTS

PART ONE

Introduction	8
Into the Shadows	12
Pathways to Joy	19
Surprised by Joy	24
Peace Process	28
Prayer Cells	31
A Place in the Sun	36
Healing Love	38
Elsa's Story	42
East-End Boy	46
Brief Encounters	55
Anne Marie's Story	59
Wendy's Story	63
Learning to Forgive	67
When Love Breaks Through	71
All at Sea	75
A Bowl of Cherries	79
A Battle Won	81
John's Story	83
An Extraordinary Life	88
A New Beginning	93
Margaret's Story	96
"Got Any Bread?"	104
Serendipities	108
In Tandem with God	112
Timeless Moments	114

PART TWO

Preamble   119
Letters to My Love   124

PART THREE

Fear No Evil   171
Valley of Shadows   175
The Divine Embrace   180
The Final Test   183

PART FOUR

Points to Ponder   191
Spring of Joy   203
Footnote   205

PART ONE

INTRODUCTION

When I was in my teens, my secret ambition was to write fiction. I think that even in those days I sensed that this particular art form was a means of conveying truth. Yet the very idea of this seems to be a contradiction in terms. How can "made-up" stories about things that never really happened be anything more than a form of amusement or entertainment? But Jesus actually used parables – in other words, stories based on His experience of life – to embody His teachings. There were over forty in all, among them the story of the Prodigal son, which one literary critic once acclaimed as the best short story ever written.

Matthew says: 'All this Jesus said to the crowds in parables . . . and this was to fulfil what was spoken by the prophet: "I will open my mouth in parables. I will utter what has been hidden since the foundation of the world."' This seems to me to confirm the idea that truth can be very effectively conveyed through fiction, and explains why the meaning of Jesus' parables went straight to the heart of the listening people. They could identify with the characters, and would instantly respond to Jesus' knowledge of human nature.

When I actually began to write fiction, I was constantly looking out for ideas to use as plots for my stories. I gathered my ideas from real life, taking care to camouflage any details which might offend people I knew. But there came a time when I found myself gripped by a story I read in *Readers' Digest* – the story of a little girl who had died of leukaemia. I was so moved by this article, that I tore the page out of the magazine and put it away for future consideration. I began to plan a novel which would depict how a Christian family coped with such a tragedy.

What I did not know was that at the very time of filing away that article, my own nine-year-old daughter had the seeds of that same disease in her body. A year later, she would be dead.

The book that came out of this experience was my first non-fictional one. It was called *Beyond the Shadows* and was to touch the hearts of thousands of people in a way that I could never have dreamed of. People wrote to tell me that the intimacy with which I had told my tragic, yet triumphant story, had enabled them to enter into the experience themselves and identify with our family's heartache. As a result, some told how they had come into a new relationship with God through reading the book. The knowledge that blessing had come to so many people through Frankie's story shone like a rainbow over the darkness of what had happened to us.

In this new book I have traced the way in which seemingly impossible situations have enabled people to find new pathways to a life of joy and fulfilment. All the stories here are true ones, and although some of them are from my own experience, many are not. They have been told to me by friends and contacts, all of whom are glad of an opportunity to share with others what God has done for them.

There are some very moving stories here and it is hoped that every reader will be blessed by reading them. We are so grateful to everyone who has been willing to share themselves with us in this way. For whereas fictional stories, or parables, can teach us many lessons we might not learn by any other means, a true story takes us right into the experience of another person, and gives us the privilege of sharing something very precious.

The second part of this book consists of extracts from a journal I kept after the sudden death of my husband. I have included this in the hope that it will help others to cope with their own grieving process. At the time, I found the exercise of recording my feelings to be very therapeutic, and I would recommend the idea to anyone else who is struggling to come to terms with the loss of a loved one. The way in which God made Himself known to me during this time, giving me at times an actual awareness of spiritual joy, is something that I now feel able to share with others.

Part Three follows my journey through a recent battle with cancer, a journey which took me through totally unfamiliar territory, but which enabled me to experience once more the sustaining love and grace of God. The joy which had been a hallmark of my Christian life thus far, in spite of deep trials and dark interludes, was sorely tested during this time, but I have emerged with that fundamental sense of spiritual joy intact. To me this particular fruit of the Spirit is perhaps the most precious.

The book ends with a selection of quotations from a personal anthology, compiled during the course of my life from a wide variety of reading material. They have been a source of enrichment to me, and I hope they will be a blessing to others.

The Scriptures radiate with references to Christian joy, many of them well-loved and familiar to believers everywhere. We are continually being promised that joy follows weeping, that sorrow will be turned to joy, that those who sow in tears will reap with joy. Jesus spoke of the fullness of joy which is His gift to those who follow Him and the epistles ring with the music of heavenly joy.

When I came to look up all the many references to joy in my concordance, I found this lovely introductory paragraph, attributed to Dr W. M. Clow, the editor:

> In no other religion and in no other literature is joy so conspicuous as in Christianity and in the Bible. Physically and psychologically speaking, it is the criterion of health

whereby all the powers and affections are enriched and harmonised. So in religion it denotes the satisfaction of the soul at attaining its desire; and Christianity stands firm so long as men who have it are invested with joy.

INTO THE SHADOWS

There had been – as there always seems to be nowadays – some trouble abroad. The papers were full of accounts of brutalities and violent death. As always, the innocent had suffered with the guilty, and suffering now engulfed yet another section of struggling humanity. As I had often asked myself before – what if any of these things should happen to me? I thought of missionaries who suffered and died at the hands of the very people they had sacrificed all to evangelize. Could anything take away the terror from the heart of a man or woman who knew that, at any moment, death – and brutal death at that – would strike? How could being a Christian make any real difference? How could it? After all, pain was pain. If you hit your head on the wall hard enough, it hurt – nothing could alter that. And if your husband or child died, then grief would strike you down. How could being a Christian make any difference, fundamentally, to that? Little did I realize then how my questions were to be answered.

Looking back now across the years to the bitter experience of losing our younger daughter to leukaemia, a host of poignant memories crowd into my mind.

I am standing in a hospital corridor outside the ward where Frankie lay, waiting for doctors to emerge with their diagnosis. I hear one of them say: 'And what is the prognosis?' I am visiting on my own that day, as Arthur is unable to be with me. I have promised to ring him as soon as there is any news.

The two white-coated doctors approach me. They open the door of a small side-room, and motion for me to follow them inside. The gravity of their expressions tell me that the news is not good. The hope that the persistent pain which Frankie has been experiencing in her legs might be attributed to nothing more serious than arthritis seems now to be unlikely. I wait anxiously for the specialist in charge of Frankie's case to speak.

'As you know', he says eventually, 'we have been rather puzzled by Frances' symptoms. There have been a number of things which didn't seem to fit. But finally, having given her a special test, I'm afraid I have some serious news for you. She has leukaemia.' My blood runs cold, but after a while, I hear myself say in a low, but calm voice:

'There isn't anything you can do for that, is there?' My question seems to relieve the tension in the room. The specialist explains brightly that treatment will begin straightaway with some 'wonderful drugs which we can give.'

'But the effect will be only temporary, won't it? I mean, in the end, nothing will be any good will it?' I am now well acquainted with all the facts from that *Reader's Digest* article. 'Please tell me – how long will it be?'

Now the specialist leans back in his chair and looks me straight in the eye.

'Six months', he says. 'A year – maybe even two. And in the meantime, who knows what may come up. We're working on this thing, you know – all the time!'

My memory of this moment is that if I had been told that Frankie could only live for a few days, it would have been easier to bear. But to be told that the heartbreaking journey toward almost inevitable death might take up to two years was more than I could bear. Soon

I was sharing the news with Arthur, and we were holding each other in a silent embrace. It was, indeed the beginning of an agonising journey – a year which would take us through a whole range of contrasting emotions and experiences.

Yet, paradoxically, I can only remember the weeks that followed as a time of golden sunshine, both in regard to the weather and to our family happiness. When she first came out of hospital, Frankie asked for a pictorial dictionary. She spent hours sitting in her wheelchair in the garden, turning up words, reading their meaning and writing lists of all the different kinds of fish, or dogs or monkeys. or whatever . . .

'Isn't life interesting, Mummy!' she said. Her bright blue eyes twinkled and shone with irrepressible merriment. She said the same thing when x-rays or blood tests were being taken later: 'Isn't this interesting?'

As a family, we were determined to enjoy the times that we spent together. Sometimes we would all have a day by the sea.

'Let's go on the pier!' Frankie would say. 'Let's all go and have a good giggle!'

She loved the crazy mirrors on the pier at Brighton. In fact, she liked anything that was good for a hearty laugh. Life was good – life was for living . . .

We decided that it would not be wise to tell Elizabeth how severely ill Frankie was.

We began to pray for a miracle. Someone suggested that we take her to Crowhurst Healing Centre for the laying on of hands. We began to study all the New Testament had to teach us about healing, and despair gave way to excitement. One day, when she was in a lot of pain, Frankie had said: 'If Jesus were here He would only have to walk into the room and lay hands on me, and I'd be better!' Now, at Crowhurst, the four of us were bowing our heads in believing prayer while sensitive, dedicated hands were laid on our heads. It was a precious moment. As we drove away down the narrow country lanes. our hearts were full of a sense of quiet exaltation.

'I ought to be able to leap and run, like the lame man at the Beautiful Gate' remarked Frankie. 'Perhaps I will when I get home.'

She was leaping and running before very long, and by September she was ready to go back to school. But the improvement lasted only a few weeks. Soon, a high dose of steroids was necessary, and our slim, fragile little daughter began to change in appearance so much that her friends did not recognize her. This gross increase in weight was one of the hardest things to bear. When I bathed her, I choked back the horror I felt at the sight of her grotesquely swollen body. But Frankie herself seemed quite happy with her new image, and I took comfort from that. Besides, she looked so well at this time that I knew it was foolish to fret.

As the illness wore on, we had no doubt whatever that God was making Himself very real and close to Frankie herself. Her serenity and courage, especially toward the end, could not be explained by anything as simple as a cheerful disposition, or a mere childlike acceptance of the inevitable. To her, the prayer-time we had each night was as essential as the meals she ate. She spoke calmly and naturally about Jesus, and about prayer. There was a strange detachment about her, as though she were already moving in a different dimension from the rest of us.

This was certainly not due to any specially 'angelic' quality in Frankie herself, for part of the extreme lovableness of her personality was that she was always so down to earth, so open and spontaneous in all that she did and said. She had a definite will of her own, and could be as difficult as any other normal child when she wanted to assert it. But people who saw her during her times of special weakness commented that she seemed to be surrounded by some other 'presence'.

One day she said: 'Some words just keep on singing themselves into my mind: Because Jesus died for me, He'll take care of me, all the way.' We looked in vain for a hymn or a chorus which said just these words. We could only conclude it was the voice of God speaking comfort and assurance to her fearful little heart. She often played hymns on her recorder, and one of my most precious memories is of seeing her sitting on the hearth rug just before that last Christmas, singing 'Away in a Manger . . . I've never been able to sing that carol since. When she had finished singing it, she climbed up on my knee and pressed her hot little cheek to mine.

We went to Essex for Christmas, and she enjoyed all the usual traditional things – the parties, the games, the presents – and the meeting up with cousins, aunts and uncles. We played charades, and there was all the fun of dressing up. But nothing could hide the knowledge that all was not well. Her painful journey was coming to an end. After the games, most of the children in the family gave some little performance of something they could do, and Frankie played her recorder. A photograph of this reminds me of the thinly veiled tension in the room as relatives who had seen very little of her during the preceding months watched her play.

I suppose the time that Frankie spent in the Royal Alexandra Hospital for Sick Children in Brighton was, for us all, the most distressing period of that whole year. Yet, looking back to those days now we remember, not the tragedy, but the triumph – not the mental suffering, but the peace that passes understanding which was ours at that time.

On the face of it, such experience is quite illogical. How can human beings undergoing the extreme stresses and strains of family tragedies such as ours know peace of mind – and even joy? Questions like this had niggled at my mind for weeks before Frankie had become ill. So many questions – so many of them unanswered . . . Now I knew – not because I had been convinced by arguments, but because God had stepped right into the very centre of my life and made the experience my own.

One night when Frankie was begging me not to leave her, she flung her arms round my neck, imploring me not to go. All around us were other children with various kinds of sickness. A young lad called Nicky was preparing to go home for the week-end. He was putting on a new pair of trousers, and the label was still on the back. I knew that he was in the last stages of leukaemia. Little Kim had been in a coma for several weeks. Her grieving parents spent hours just sitting by her bed.

It was a heart-breaking place to be. I had been sleeping in the hospital, but now needed to go home for a couple of days to look after the needs of the rest of the family. As I tried to say goodbye to her, Frankie began to stroke my face, feeling my mouth, my chin, my hair. 'All these other children', she said, 'can't possibly love their mothers as much as I love you. They can't possibly. Please, please don't leave me . . .'

It was a dark moment, a moment of temporary despair. How much more could I bear? I walked, later, down to the beach and stood by the water's edge, and I poured out my heart in prayer for the suffering world, for the sick children in the ward I had just left. For Nicky in his new trousers going home to die. For little Kim and her grieving parents. For my own little one, who had begged me not to leave. Once more I needed to reach deeply into the well where God's peace was available. Later there would be joy, too. But not now. Not at that moment of grief . . .

Logically, I knew I should be feeling at the end of my tether, and in some ways I was. The emotional upheaval of the morning had left me feeling weak and drained. Yet, in spite of this I experienced now a sudden upsurge of serenity. God was so close in that moment, I felt I could have put out a hand and touched Him. 'Closer than breathing, nearer than hands and feet.'

All the way through, Arthur had been quite wonderful, standing up in the pulpit to preach every Sunday, and coming back indoors to go straight to Frankie's side. Only that previous Sunday he had preached on the greatness of God:

'When you are losing your grip, exhausted with anxiety, burdened beyond endurance – when all earthly props have gone, then He gives strength. "They that wait upon the Lord shall renew their strength, they shall mount up with wings as eagles. they shall run and not faint . . ."'

Not long before she died, we took Frankie up to the top of Ditchling Beacon where we could look out on to the glorious vista of the Sussex Weald. We ate our picnic, and Elizabeth with some other friends ran down the hillside, enjoying the feeling of the wind on their faces and in their hair. From the safety of the car, Frankie looked on. Then after a moment, she said: 'I wish I could run like that!'

For a moment we could not answer. Then: 'You will, my darling, you will,' I heard myself saying. And an inner voice added: "If not on these hills, then on the golden hills of heaven.'

Why was our prayer for healing not granted? Many people have asked that question. But it does not have an answer. Frankie herself did not ask the question. One day I had. found a note on the kitchen table, written in her childish scrawl: 'Dear Mummy, I love you very much.' Arthur found a similar one on his desk: 'Dear Daddy, I love you.'

On her coffin, we placed her little red Bible, open at her favourite passage – Psalm 23.

PATHWAYS TO JOY

When I sat down to write the story of my daughter's death shortly after the ordeal was over, I described the days immediately preceding the end in these words: 'I remember waking up each morning, after a restless night, and feeling joy literally flooding my heart. Beside me, the laboured breathing of my precious child told me that she was still with us. And I lifted up my heart to God in praise for yet another day in which to love and serve her'. . .

When I came to prepare the final draft of the manuscript for publication, I altered the word 'joy' to 'peace', because I was afraid that readers who had never passed through such an experience might misunderstand and be shocked that any mother was capable of feeling joy at such a time as this. In retrospect, I am surprised myself. The experience now seems unreal, out of this world – as, of course, it was. Yet reading through the words I wrote at the time, I am able to taste again, in a measure, that 'miracle of joy'.

But little did I know at the time that my personal journey through the valley of shadows had only just begun. The years which immediately followed Frankie's death were filled with opportunities to bring blessing to others – initially through writing the story down, and then through many opportunities to speak publicly about the question of suffering.

But there was some bitter fruit to follow, for when she was in her early twenties our elder daughter succumbed to a mental illness which was subsequently to affect us all deeply for many years. People often asked us how Elizabeth had coped with her sister's illness, since they noticed that she was rarely mentioned in the story I had written. The reason for this was that Elizabeth had been unable to share her feelings with us, and admitted later that she had buried them away inside, as the pain of them was too deep to bear. Unfortunately, the result of this was to give everyone the impression that all was well. Elizabeth had friends of her own, loved being out in the countryside with a farming family who had access to horses, and we took pleasure in fitting her out with riding gear so that she could enjoy taking part in local gymkhanas.

But underneath this façade of 'normal' living, an undercurrent of negative emotions was building up. Our daughter felt isolated and misunderstood, resentful of all the attention which was being lavished on her sick sister, and unable to give any kind of expression to her inner confusion. The teen-age years – difficult enough at any time for most people – were overshadowed by secret feelings of inadequacy and insecurity. When she moved away from home to begin her nursing training, her problems increased, until finally a complete mental breakdown overtook her

What followed is too private and painful to record, and for twenty-five years we struggled, as a family to cope with the effects of this terrible illness – an illness which brings with it so much pain and misunderstanding for all concerned. P.D. James, the crime writer has expressed so well the dilemma faced by those who care for the mentally ill in her autobiography *Time to be Earnest*:

> Only those who have lived with the mental illness of someone they love can understand what this entails. One suffers with the patient and for oneself. Another human

being who was once a beloved companion can become not only a stranger, but occasionally a malevolent stranger. It is easy sometimes to understand why mental illness was once seen as possession by an evil spirit . . .

Throughout the years which followed the initial breakdown, there were periods when Elizabeth responded to the various treatments she underwent, and each time this happened we clung to the hope that healing had taken place. To maintain our faith in these circumstances was sometimes well nigh impossible. Yet beneath all the despair and darkness there shone, for me, a promise that God would ultimately reveal Himself in a way that we could not foresee. And underneath this persistent assurance there was joy – a spring of joy that I knew could never be quenched. When healing did finally come for Elizabeth that joy was complete, and my only sadness was that my husband never lived to see the transformation of his beloved daughter.

Later, I was to say that the pain we suffered during those twenty-five years was more terrible than the year we spent nursing Frankie through her terminal sickness. For the person who is drawn periodically into the horror of mental illness lives in a land of dark distortion and is unable to give or receive any kind of love. And this, surely, constitutes a kind of hell. This kind of suffering is incommunicable.

In circumstances like these then, where do the precious gifts of peace and joy come from, and how can we attain them? The secret, surely, is in Jesus Christ Himself, who appeals to His followers to "abide" in Him, that His peace may garrison their hearts and minds, and that their joy may be full. The fruits of the Spirit often take us by surprise, simply because they are not of our own making. Like the "peace that passes understanding" the joy that sits side by side with sorrow and grief in the human heart is God-given. It has lit the faces of the martyrs down the ages, rung out like bells in the voices of those who have faced persecution for naming the Name of Christ, and shone like a light in the darkest corners of the earth.

Sabina Wurmbrand, tells of the seven nightmare years she spent in Communist prisons and labour camps. The unimaginable sufferings of those years make the average Western mind shrink from even having to contemplate them. Interrogations, beatings, starvation and slave labour sent some women mad, while others succumbed to merciful death. Sabina was a shining witness to Christ in the dungeons and rat infested shacks where the women lived like animals. In moments of special terror, other women clung to her like children to a mother, feeling a pathetic sense of safety in being able to touch someone in whom the Spirit of God so obviously dwelt.

Not knowing whether her husband – who was a prisoner elsewhere, and for whose sake she herself was being held – was alive or dead; not having seen her young son since he was nine years old, this woman could nevertheless speak faithfully of Christ and of her trust in Him. When she was eventually released, her son – now a tall teenage lad – asked her: 'How could you bear all this without giving way and denying Christ?'

Sabina answered by telling him of a peculiarity in the Hebrew language where some future events are described in the perfect tense. The fifty–third chapter of Isaiah, for example, foretells the sufferings of the Messiah, but speaks of these events as belonging to the past, not the future. When Jesus was already on the path of suffering, He would have read of these events as if they had already happened.

Sabina explained: 'Joy is the everlasting present of the Christian spirit. I was in a heavenly place from which no one could move me. Where was the affliction through which I passed? To that most inviolable part of my mind, it belonged to the past. I lived the suffering long ago, while the present reality was delight in the closeness of the Lord.'

Such thoughts are only to be found, fathoms deep, on the ocean bed of Christian experience.

I once heard the late Malcolm Muggeridge talking about Pastor Bonhoeffer, who was executed by the Nazis for refusing to renounce his faith. As he faced death, it is said that Bonhoeffer's whole countenance shone with a radiance which confounded his executioners.

'In that place of darkest evil', said Malcolm Muggeridge, 'he was the happiest man – he, the executed. I find this an image of supreme happiness.'

With all due respect to Malcolm Muggeridge, I would prefer to describe the radiance that shone from the martyr's face as 'joy' 'Happiness' is a word used to describe something transitory, something dependent on our circumstances. Joy, however is an irrepressible effluence which has its source in the indwelling Christ. Joy is alive; joy is creative; joy is infectious. It is a light which cannot be put out by sorrow, by adversity, or by persecution. Joy is a miracle because it is a fruit of the Spirit of God Himself.

SURPRISED BY JOY

C. S. Lewis wrote a book about his own spiritual journey from atheism to Christianity and called it *Surprised by Joy*. But Lewis himself had to tread a very painful path later on in his life which made him rethink many of the things he had written so confidently about in his younger days.

Although I suppose its true to say that many people get acquainted with Lewis by means of his fictional works, notably the children's Narnia stories, I was one who did it the other way around. Having read *Mere Christianity*, *The Problem of Pain*, etc., it was only later that I discovered this great scholar also wrote for children. I have to say that I sometimes felt there was a kind of ruthless logic about much of his writing which sometimes made me cringe. For me it was an almost remorseless logic and I found myself inwardly protesting at times against the coldness of it. Secretly, I felt that if the great professor had been married and had a family of his own, he might have written rather differently.

But there came a time when, to the amazement of his friends and colleagues, Lewis did, in fact, enter into an extraordinary relationship with a woman. That woman was Joy Davidman, an American divorcee, with whom he had been corresponding for sometime. When they eventually met, Joy invaded the Oxford Don's strictly bachelor existence in such a way that he was never to be quite the same again.

'Her mind was lithe and quick and muscular as a leopard', he wrote later. Passion, tenderness and pain were all equally unable to disarm it . . .' Her intellect fascinated him. 'It scented the first whiff of cant or slush; then sprang and knocked you over before you knew what was happening. How many bubbles of mine she pricked!...'

Although Joy was certainly not liked by a number of Lewis's friends, they said, after visiting him later: 'Jack seemed very different: much more muted, gentle and relaxed. Even his voice and laugh seemed quieter. . .' They felt that his sensitive nature had at last come through.'

It is surely more than a coincidence that Lewis called his autobiography, which he was just completing when he met Joy, *Surprised by Joy*, because this little phrase must have had more than one aspect of meaning for him at the time! After her subsequent illness and death, Lewis wrote this:

> The most precious gift that marriage gave me was this constant impact of something very close and intimate, yet all the time unmistakably 'other'. Is all that work to be undone? Is what I shall still call Joy to sink back horribly into being not much more than one of my old bachelor pipe–dreams? Oh, God, God, why did you take such trouble to force this creature out of its shell if it is doomed to crawl back – to be sucked back – into it?

The book that Lewis wrote following his wife's death shocked many people who came to read it later. He called it *A Grief Observed* and wrote it under a pen name, so it was quite a while before his regular readers discovered who the author actually was. It was a book in which he gave expression to all his grief, his pain and his anger against God.

Where is God? Go to him when your need is desperate, when all other help is vain, and what do you find? A door slammed in your face, and a sound of bolting and double bolting on the inside. After that, silence. You may as well turn away. The longer you wait, the more emphatic the silence will become. There are no lights in the windows. It might be an empty house. Was it ever inhabited? It seemed so once, and that 'seeming' was as strong as this. What can it mean? Why is God so present a commander in our time of prosperity and so very absent a help in time of trouble?

No wonder Lewis first brought out this book under an assumed name. He knew just how much it would shock his regular readers. And, of course it did, once the true identity of the author was revealed. But by this time C. S. Lewis himself had died. By pouring out his grief in this way, and allowing all the bitter feelings to be aired, he no doubt felt a measure of relief. 'The more we believe that God hurts only to heal', he writes, 'the less we can believe that there is any use in begging for tenderness . . .'

It comes as a great relief to the reader, as the heart-rending journal nears its end, to find an abating of the inner rage, a kind of calm after the storm: 'I have gradually been coming to feel' he writes, 'that the door is no longer shut and bolted. Was it my own frantic need that slammed it in my face? The time when there is nothing at all in your soul except a cry for help may be just the time when God can't give it: you are like a drowning man who can't be helped because he clutches and grabs. Perhaps your own cries deafen you to the voice you hoped to hear.'

Grief is perhaps the hardest exercise in trust any of us are asked to undergo.

'I'm trying to pray' said one recently widowed woman. 'But I can't, because I'm so angry with God for taking my husband away from me.'

Like C. S. Lewis, it is possible to shout so loud at God, to hammer so loudly at the door asking for an explanation, that we are deaf to His voice, and immune from His healing love. When Mary Magdalene stood in the garden of resurrection, her eyes blinded by tears of grief, she could not see Jesus standing there. But when she heard Him speak her name, she fell at His feet, knowing she was face to face with the Lord of life and of love. And it was then that she experienced real joy.

PEACE PROCESS

An Irishwoman sat sobbing in her brother's house. She had just heard that her son had been given a total of forty-four years' imprisonment for a series of crimes connected with terrorism.

'There's no hope for him!' cried the mother. 'He's so caught up in all this violence that he'd go straight back into it if he was released! This is his third prison sentence, and he'll never change. He's just a hopeless case.'

Her brother tried in vain to comfort her. But there was another person in the room, someone who was not a member of the family. She was an old lady of eighty-three, and she sat quietly watching the distressing scene. Then, quietly, she spoke:

'That's not true. Your son is not a hopeless case. God can change him. There is hope!'

The mother just smiled wearily.

'I shall pray for your David every day', insisted the older woman. 'I shall pray that God will change his heart!'

David had become involved in the troubles of Northern Ireland when he was sixteen, and at seventeen had decided to join the Protestant para-military group. Angry at the way the IRA terrorists seemed so often to get off scot-free, he took up the loyalist cause. One thing led to another, until he himself became deeply involved in terrorism. He vowed that, if necessary, he would die for Ulster.

Now, facing forty-four years' in prison, bitter and hardened by his crimes, he sat one day in his cell, drinking a cup of tea. It was just over a year since that old lady had started to pray that God would change his heart, and he, of course, knew nothing about that. As he sipped his tea, his eyes fell on a tract which somebody had left on his bed. He glanced at it, then threw it out of the window in disgust.

Then a strange thing happened. As he sat down again to drink his tea, a thought began to hammer into the back of his mind. Where it came from he could not think . . . but, there it was – thumping away in his head, and demanding his attention. The thought was, quite simply, that he should become a Christian.

'This is terrible', he said to himself. 'Why am I thinking like this? Someone has put dope into my tea!'

Then his glance fell on the Bible, a copy of which was in every cell.

'Even if I wanted to, I couldn't become a Christian', he muttered. 'I'm too bad. God just wouldn't be interested.'

He grinned as he remembered how every prisoner likes his Bible for one reason only! He had used it to make cigarette papers, like everybody else did. He had smoked Matthew, Mark, Luke and John; but now he took the Bible off the shelf and started to read some of the verses on the fly-pages – verses which had been specially selected for those in need of help.

'For God so loved the world', he read . . . 'That must be for good people – not for the likes of me!'

Then he found himself reviewing his life, remembering how many times he had been spared, and how many times the IRA had tried to kill him. Once he was almost killed by a bomb he himself had been planting – in a building which caught fire while he was still in it. Why should God have kept him alive? Why had he been spared?

At last he went down on his knees, begging God to change him, and to take away the violence and bitterness from his heart. And then the miracle which the old lady had prayed for took place.

David became a radiant witness to the saving grace of God in that prison, and eventually saw over a hundred men become Christians. A politician who came to visit the prison was amazed to see IRA and UDA prisoners sitting side-by-side studying their Bibles. Speechless, he walked out. But later he was reported to have said this:

'Some of the best brains in England have been trying to find a solution to the troubles in Northern Ireland. But today I have seen a solution that nobody will believe!'

And somewhere in Ireland, an old lady was quietly praising God for yet another answer to her prayers For throughout her life she had proved many times that in God's sight there is no such thing as a hopeless case.

PRAYER CELLS

Another heart-warming story of prison life is told by Jonathan Aitken, in his book, *Porridge and Passion*. The ex-government minister who served time in HM Prison, Belmarsh after he had been convicted of perjury, told part of his story in a book he wrote prior to his prison sentence. *Pride and Perjury* chronicles the whole bitter experience of his fall from grace. But it also tells how God met with him in an extraordinary way, initially through being invited to an Alpha course by a friend.

Following a session on the Holy Spirit, Jonathan writes:

> Despite all the impact this manifestation had on me, I cannot pretend that my life changed overnight. I did not think I had been 'saved', or that I had had some blinding light on the road to Damascus. Indeed, in immediate retrospect, I felt that my encounter with the force that had shaken me to the core was as much an unnerving experience as an uplifting one. I decided to think and pray about it.

What actually happened was that Jonathan felt prompted to seek further help by making a full confession to a trusted Anglican priest.

He writes very movingly of this experience, saying that it was much too private and profound to share with others. 'But the sense of joyful release that flooded over me afterwards was glorious.' Having laid all his past burdens of animosity at the foot of the Cross, before coming to kneel there to ask forgiveness for his own sins, he knew that something momentous had happened.

'Somewhere along the painful road of the journey, after many months of prayer and listening, my eyes opened and I recognized that I had accepted Jesus Christ into my heart as my Lord and my God.'

So it came about that Jonathon's entry into Belmarsh Prison to commence his sentence took place in the most unusual of circumstances. It was the beginning of another extraordinary chapter in his life. He tells how he awoke on the first morning, wondering how he would survive the coming day. It was 5.30 a.m. and he still had, ringing in his ears, the sound of an obscene chant which had greeted his arrival the day before. The theme of the chant had been 'Let's get Aitken tomorrow!'

His blood had run cold when he heard raucous exchanges from the exercise yard, accompanied by a thunder of unprintable responses. But having read a Psalm and sent up some desperate prayers for help, he had fallen asleep and awaked with a strange sense of peace. Looking around his cell, he felt he could just about understand how monks down the ages had found cells good places in which to pray!

But what did the day hold, and how about all those threats of the night before? He was still praying, when he was interrupted by shouts of 'Unlock! Everybody out!'

As he stepped out of his cell, he remembered that the noisiest vocalists of the night before had been his immediate neighbours to his right and left. So he trembled as he stood on the landing beside them. But what had happened? Where had all the hostility gone?

'Morning', said one of them. 'Hope you slept well. Sorry about last night. We were on the tackle [drugs]. Just letting off steam.'

'Yeah, nothing personal mate', said another. Then they invited him to have a cup of tea with them at break time! Jonathan soon discovered that underneath the surface of these outwardly macho young men lurked a lot of human vulnerability. On the second day of his sentence, a young black prisoner came up to Jonathan and asked him to read a letter for him. It was a letter from the prisoner's brief, but he could neither read or write. Jonathan helped him sort out the contents of the letter, and then wrote a reply for him. The young man skipped away holding the envelope above his head and shouting: 'That MP geezer's got fantastic joined up writing!'

Soon, Jonathan was in much demand. And found himself reading and writing all kind of letters. One day an Irish burglar invited him to his cell for coffee and made a little speech of thanks. 'On behalf of the lads, I'd really like to thank you for all the letter writing you've done for us. And I'd like to give you a present to say how much we appreciate it. So you can have anything you like from me library!'

Paddy then dived underneath his bed and brought up an amazing selection of hardcore porn magazines. Startled, Jonathan declined the offer as politely as he could. Paddy was puzzled, but quickly dived under the other side of his bed. 'If it's the boys you're after', he began . . .

'No, no', said Jonathan hurriedly. 'I used to like the first kind you showed me. But these days I'm trying a different path in life.'

'So what kind of path would that be?'

'Well, if you really want to know . . .' And he explained that it was a path of prayer and obedience to the teachings of Jesus Christ. 'it's a path that has changed my life.'

A long silence followed, and it was eventually broken by Paddy.

'You know, I'd really like to try that path myself.' Then he poured out his heart there in the prison cell. 'There's no meaning to my life . . . no point to it all . . . my relationships keep going wrong . . . my life's just empty and totally unfulfilled.'

Jonathan had vowed never to talk about religion while in jail. 'Jesus freaks often get beaten up', he'd been told. But now he realized he had to respond to Paddy.

When he suggested they prayed together, his offer was immediately taken up. They ended up praying together for the next three nights.

Paddy then went off and recruited two or three friends to join them, and before they knew where they were, twelve young men were meeting regularly for prayer, and for sharing their needs and questions. Jonathan says that, far from being the tutor for the group, he became the beneficiary. Because these men just prayed from their hearts, pouring everything out without embarrassment.

Some of the young men would address their prayers to God the Father, not least because they had never known the love of an earthly father. Others prayed to God the Son because they knew they needed to relate to Jesus and what He offered – compassion, forgiveness, healing and a love for sinners 'Others prayed for the power of the Holy Spirit to come in and transform their lives, so that they could turn away from crime, drugs, anger, and other demons. This was spiritual life in the raw, stripping away many of my own protective defences', says Jonathan. 'Things which had separated me from God and my neighbours in the past.'

The result was that, as he looked back to the time he spent in prison, Jonathon could see that he had actually grown as a Christian during those years. He had learned to regard his fellow prisoners with compassion and understanding, and had been humble enough to learn from them too.

And perhaps the most important lessons he had learned were

about prayer, and about the way in which the love of God reaches out to anyone who reaches out to Him. He saw men's lives being changed, but he also felt his own life changing too. What he actually gained from his life as a convict he later realised to be far more fulfilling than the prizes of public life as a Cabinet minister.

'I can now say from my heart', he says: 'Thank you, God, for sending me to prison.'

A PLACE IN THE SUN

A place in the sun. That's a phrase which has more than one meaning. In a world where there is so much heartache and inner conflict, so much secret loneliness and disillusionment, Christians surely have something very precious to share with others. All around are folk who seem to be longing for a spiritual dimension to life, who are turning away from the materialism of our age, and looking for something which will bring warmth and meaning into the bleakness of their everyday lives. In a way, it is as though they are shivering in a kind of winter of the spirit. They reach out their hands to warm themselves by any fire they can find – and often get burnt.

The story of how John Bunyan first came to discover Jesus Christ for himself is a simple, yet moving one. There came a time in his life when, after hearing a particularly challenging sermon, he began to read his Bible seriously for the first time. He found at first that certain texts made him turn inwards on himself in bitter condemnation. He could not find the joy he longed for.

Then one day, as he was out walking, he saw a group of women from the local church congregation sitting outside their cottages in the sun. And as he passed by, he could hear that they were talking about the things of God. The joy on their faces and the excitement in their voices drew him so forcibly that he was filled with a longing to share whatever it was these women possessed. He saw that they were actually alive with the knowledge of God.

Later, Bunyan wrote about them like this:

> I saw the happiness of these people as if they were on the sunny side of some high mountain, therefore refreshing themselves with the pleasant beams of the sun, while I was shivering and shrinking in the cold. Methought, also, betwixt me and them, I saw a wall that did compass about this mountain. Now through this wall my soul did greatly desire to pass, concluding that if it could, I would go even into the very midst of them, and there also comfort myself with the heat of their sun . . .

In the archaic beauty of these words, I find a timely challenge. And I ask myself, do people really long to come into the heat of my sun? The simple witness of those women several hundred years ago almost certainly played its part in what was to follow in John Bunyan's life, and no doubt contributed to the inspiration for the eventual writing of *The Pilgrims Progress*. And who can judge the incalculable fruit that has come out of that classic story ?

HEALING LOVE
(As told by Caroline)

'Quickly – under the table, children! The helicopters are here again! They have just touched down at the bottom of the garden, and the soldiers inside are pointing their machine guns straight at our window!'

I didn't hear them come down, and I'm sure I didn't see anyone holding a gun, but they must be there, mum says they are. We hastily fall to the floor, and then crawl underneath the kitchen table, hoping we will now be safe from the snipers outside. I am one of five children, and we crouch, shaking and petrified, waiting patiently for the sound of machine gun fire. I am seven years old.

The weeks drag by after that particular incident, when suddenly, in the depth of the night, when we are sound asleep, the lights in our bedroom come on, and I hear mum screaming:

'Hurry, we are being gassed! The gas is being pumped through the bathroom window. Downstairs, as fast as you can!'

I have never run so fast in my life, and at the same time I try to concentrate on my breathing. Can I still breathe? I have heard somewhere that gas can kill you. Are we all going to die? Terror grips me. Where can we hide?

Next, our house was infested with Colorado beetles, and the

police were called out to investigate. They searched the house from top to bottom, but, of course, they found nothing.

There were gunmen who lived in the flats opposite our house. So our curtains had to be drawn all the time, day and night. We never saw daylight while we were in the house, and the gunmen couldn't see us. As a small child, I was kept inside the house by my mother, so that no harm from the outside world would come to me. I felt safer with my mum than I did with the rest of the world.

Soon, my dad was seen as the enemy. He became a murderer and a sex offender. How does my mum know all these things? Are we safe with dad in the house? Looking back, I marvel that I survived such a childhood. The situations I have described were only hallucinations and visions that my mum constantly experienced, but to her, and to myself as a child, they were very real: they were actually happening. I believed everything my mother said. There were to be ten years of bizarre and strange happenings before the family was told she was a schizophrenic. But her diagnosis meant nothing to me. It didn't change anything.

Time and time again mum was sent into a mental hospital due to the extremity of her illness. There was no-one to explain her illness to me. School was a nightmare. I would sit and stare out of the classroom window, just waiting for a taxi to turn up with my mum being the passenger. She would often escape from the hospital wearing only a nightdress, and with nothing on her feet. She would ask the headmaster to come and fetch me from class, and as he did so I would hear sniggers from the other children, who had seen it all happen before.

I hated the way my mum was, and even though I didn't know God then, I used to beg Him to take my mum's illness away and give it to me instead. School became a frightening place to be – a place where I could not learn anything, but feared everything. I even attempted to take my own life on two occasions, so desperate and hopeless did I feel.

Then someone introduced me to the Christian faith. And since becoming a believer, Jesus Christ has given me strength and power to carry on. Visiting my mother in hospital can still be a nightmare, as it is so painful. She now sees me as her enemy, and I am often attacked by her verbally – and sometimes physically. I feel strong when I am with her; but often weep bitterly when I leave. I cry for her suffering, and for the thirty years of her illness.

Some people blame God for such tragedies. But I have learned to pray constantly for the God-conscious spirit which is hidden away somewhere in my sick mother. She may never be healed physically, or mentally. But spiritually I believe there is hope. It is not easy being abused each time I visit, but I carry on in the hope that mum will see the love of Jesus in me, and will one day find Him for herself.

I do experience fear when I see my mother – fear more of the illness than of her. I have told that it can be hereditary. But I have peace of mind because I know I am in God's hands. I just pray that she will come to find peace there too.

POSTSCRIPT

Time has passed – ten years to be exact – since I wrote the above. I mentioned that my hope would be that my mother would see Jesus in me as I visited her in hospital. I believe that she has been blessed with more than a vision of Christ. She has been touched, and still is being touched, by His gentle hands of healing.

Today, after thirty years of being institutionalised, she is now in a care home within the community, able to communicate without aggression, seeing no visions of predators outside her window, and accepting me as a friend and daughter instead of someone she cannot relate to. She is quite happy to accept food and gifts freely, without the fear she once had that I was always trying to poison her.

Over the last ten years I have committed myself, with God's leading, to visit her frequently, believing that as I go in to see her, it is Jesus who goes too. There is no hostility now, for God has restored peace to her troubled mind. I have stood on the promise that He will "restore all the years that the locusts have eaten" (Joel 2:25) The Enemy has certainly taken a lot from us as a family, but, true to His Word, God is restoring. He is restoring trust, hope, peace of mind, care, comfort, faith and, yes, even my education, which had received such a battering in my childhood.

Although there are still areas in my mother's life that need the Lord's touch, I keep believing, keep hoping, keep trusting . . . And, as I visit in an attitude of prayer, keep watching for the Lord to restore ALL that the locust has eaten. And that includes the salvation of her soul.

ELSA'S STORY

'It seems a strange thing to say,' she said, 'but I can even be thankful now that I was once an alcoholic, because if I hadn't been, I would probably never have found Jesus.'

It had been one of those long, sad stories of youthful mistakes in personal relationships, leading to unhappiness, despair, and finally to the degradation that addiction of any kind brings with it. In Elsa's case, there was liberation and hope at the end of the story, for she was now a committed Christian, free from her drinking habit and keen to bear witness to what the Lord had done for her.

'You mean', I said, 'that you can be thankful because your alcoholism made you turn to the Christian faith for answers?'

'Not exactly. You see, initially it wasn't to Christ that I turned, or even to the Church. It was to Alcoholics Anonymous.'

'But they're not a specifically Christian-based organisation, are they?'

'No, they're not. But they are based on a belief in God. Do you know about the twelve steps that we all have to take – or attempt to take – when we first come to AA for help?'

I had to admit that I didn't.

'Well, first we have to admit that we are powerless over alcohol – that our lives have become unmanageable. Then we need to believe that a power greater than ourselves can restore us to sanity. We are then encouraged to turn our lives over to the care of God as we understand him.'

'So whether you were a Hindu, a Jew, a Moslem, a Jehovah's Witness, or whatever – it doesn't really matter?'

I suppose I looked sceptical, but at the same time I was growing more and more intrigued as Elsa went on describing the 'twelve steps'.

'No, not really. But wait until you hear the rest. Having "turned our wills over to God" we have to make a "searching and fearless moral inventory of ourselves, and then admit to God, to ourselves, and to another human being the exact nature of our wrongs". Does that ring any bells? What it meant in practice was that we were facing up to our sins – that is our conscious sins, of course – and admitting them, so we were then ready for the next step, which was to ask God to remove all these defects of character.'

'But as Christians we surely believe that this can only happen through faith in Jesus Christ, and His atoning work on the cross?'

'Hang on a minute while I tell you the rest!' Elsa smiled at my raised eyebrows. 'Having asked God's forgiveness, we then had to make a list of all the people we had harmed, and then make ourselves willing to make amends to them all where possible.

'But first we had to make sure that our attempt to put things right wouldn't injure another person. Having done this we are supposed to continue to make a personal inventory of our wrong-doings, and promptly admit each failure. Finally we were to try, through prayer and meditation, to improve our conscious contact with God as we understood him, praying for knowledge of His will for us, and the power to carry it out. Following these steps was said to lead to a "spiritual awakening", and we were then to carry the message to other alcoholics, and to "practice these principles in all our affairs". . .'

When Elsa finished telling me about the twelve steps, I was

amazed at how close they were to the experience of Christian conversion, and subsequent healing from deep-rooted problems.

'And does it work?' I asked.

'For many people it appears to work amazingly well', she said. 'Though the group therapy also plays a major part. The help and support of the leaders and other sufferers is vital, and I can't speak too highly of those who make AA their life's work. I certainly owe them more than I can ever say. But you see, what happened to me as I tried to take the twelve steps was this. I had no problem admitting to some of my faults, but others I found it a terrible struggle to face up to. Part of me kept on trying to justify myself, to make excuses, to blame others – it seemed desperately necessary to hold on to my self-respect in regard to my basic individuality – though I had long since lost all respect for the drink-dominated slob I had become

'And even after I had, with difficulty, made my inventory of known faults, and asked God to forgive them, I couldn't find peace of mind, somehow. I could see that the guidelines were soundly based and that they should lead to liberation, but I felt there was something vital missing from it all.

'Mind you, AA actually encourages you to look further into your own particular religion, admitting that their twelve steps can only take you so far. So I did just that. I decided to start going to church, because I had caught a glimpse of things as they ought to be, and wanted to go further.

'The first church I tried wasn't much help. They seemed to be saying much the same as AA – its up to you, take yourself in hand and get right with God. But they didn't say how! I was tired, and I was defeated, and I knew myself to powerless to kick my habit on my own. But I also seemed too be powerless to turn my will over to God as the third step advocated . . .

'It was when I got talking to a neighbour and she offered to take me to her church that things started to happen. The first sermon I heard preached brought me face to face with Jesus Christ. I was absolutely bowled over by him. Like a flash of light I saw that he was the answer, the missing link, as it were, that I had been searching for. His Spirit touched my heart, and showed me myself as I really was, then showed me Jesus dying to redeem me on the cross. I was absolutely shattered by an awareness of his love. This was the real spiritual awakening I had been waiting for. After that, I was able to take those twelve steps, but it was not "I" but the Christ who now lived in me who took me through them!'

'And what would you now have to say about AA?'

'I think it's a marvellous organisation, and I would recommend anyone with a drink problem to seek their help without hesitation. Addicts of any kind need the guidance of trained, experienced people to help them come to grips with their problem. But in the end there's only one Name 'under heaven given among men whereby we must be saved' from ourselves, and that is the Name of Jesus. And I shall love him for that for the rest of my days!'

EAST-END BOY

I first met Patrick at a church 'Quiet Day' which was being held in the home of a former Pastor. I had noticed him sitting in church with his wife Sarah, but had never really spoken to him before. I knew he had been a missionary in Japan for many years, and that he was now working as a lecturer in the Japanese department of Reading University.

On this particular day, Patrick was our main speaker. In the lunch hour we were all encouraged to move about the house and garden, either to be quiet and meditate on what we had heard so far, or to make contact with other people. Sitting in the garden not far from Patrick, I ventured to introduce myself to him. I wanted to tell him how something he had said that morning seemed to have a special relevance to my present situation.

Later, he asked me where I lived, and when I said that I was fortunate enough to rent a flat in a special complex which was reserved for retired Christian workers, he immediately showed interest. He had already heard about the flats, and now asked me if I thought there were likely to be any vacancies in the not-to-distant future, as he and Sarah would be looking for retirement accommodation soon

I promised to let him know if a vacancy should occur., and in the meantime invited him and Sarah to come and have lunch with me on the following Sunday, so that they could have some ideas of what the flats were like. The result was that some time later Patrick and Sarah became my neighbours.

I soon found out that as well as his work at the University, Patrick was in constant demand as a speaker and preacher, and travelled to many different parts of the world proclaiming the Christian message. A natural communicator, he had many stories to tell about his years in Japan and about his early years as an 'East End boy'

Born into a working class family, which at one stage consisted of nine people – his parents, three brothers, two sisters and an elderly lady who lived with them – Patrick became accustomed to all kinds of deprivation. Times were hard, and became even harder when his father injured himself at work and was forced to accept a lower paid job. His mother was so hard-pressed to make ends meet, that she stopped paying the rent. The bailiffs were called in and the whole family were evicted. For the next few years they were moved from one government-run house to another, sometimes living in just one room and making do as best they could

Patrick recalls that, in spite of everything, theirs was not an unhappy home. On the contrary, he says, like most poorer working-class families, theirs was buoyed by a constant sense of optimism. 'Humour was never far from the surface, and we were no strangers to laughter. Things were always going to take a turn for the better, and we constantly looked forward to the day when "our ship would come in"!'

There were occasional family knees up. Aunts, uncles and family friends would gather together on a Saturday night to drink, dance and sing before dropping off to sleep in odd corners all over the flat. As they got older, the children joined in this revelry, and after one such party Patrick woke up to find himself on the living room table where he had apparently spent the night.

His mother could never find enough money to keep them all properly clothed, and they would cut up cornflake packets to put into their shoes to save their socks from wearing out through the holes in their shoes. The constant economic battle eventually led to their mother's downfall. She loved her children so much that she hated to see them so poorly clothed. One day she took Patrick shopping, and to his amazement he realized she was taking articles of clothing from the shelves and slipping them into her bag. The two of them were arrested for shop-lifting. The thirteen-year-old boy was not actually charged with anything, but his mother was sentenced to six months, imprisonment. She was accused of teaching a minor how to steal.

Patrick eventually left school with four 'O' Levels and went to work as an accountant trainee at Crosse & Blackwell, where his mother had worked as a 'bean-sorter'. His success with the O Levels he puts down partly to the fact that he discovered the joy of reading just after his thirteenth birthday. He was sent to the local library to find a book for his sister, who was unwell. He decided to find one for himself – and discovered the 'Biggles' series. With the aid of a torch under the blanket, he read in bed every night, and from then on was rarely without a book to read.

Then something else happened which was eventually to change his life. Waiting for a friend one Sunday morning, he saw a man on a bicycle approaching. The man was dressed in a dark uniform, and Patrick assumed he was a policeman. When the man got off his bike and approached him, the boy began to feel very uneasy, as he had by this time been involved in all kinds of petty crime.

'What are you doing sonny?' asked the man.

'Nuffin, mister. I ain't doing nuffin!' was the defensive reply.

'Oh, good! Then why not come with me to the Boys' Brigade Bible Class?'

Thus began a completely new chapter of Patrick's life, one which was to lead him eventually to Japan. For having nothing better to do, he followed that Boys' Brigade Captain into an ancient looking mission hall where the Bible Class was held. There were about a dozen boys in the room, and according to Patrick no boy could wish to find better friends than those boys were to become to him. From the moment he stepped inside that room the pattern of his life changed completely.

He soon discovered that the Boys' Brigade had a football team, did sports training and gymnastics, played cricket and went swimming together. They also had a brass band and a weekly youth club with table tennis and snooker. Four or five times a week Patrick would be with the other boys at the mission hall. On Sundays he would be there for the Bible Class, but admits that he can remember very little of what he learned there. But the stories of St. Paul and his travels stayed in his mind. To a teenager they were thrilling tales of adventure, but it never occurred to him to wonder why Paul endured so much hardship. He thought he must have been some kind of madman to put up with all the beatings, imprisonments etc!

Then came a day which Patrick describes as a typical Saturday. In the morning he worked overtime at Crosse & Blackwell, enjoying this for the extra pocket money it brought.

But that day he was invited by a friend from the mission hall to his girl friend's birthday party. However, when he got there, he felt very disappointed. Everyone was drinking orange juice and playing 'childish games'. It was not his idea of a party at all, so he sat in a corner and read the evening paper! Then, just after ten o'clock people started to go home. The party, much to Patrick's surprise, was over!

But that night his friend John asked him to help carry a record player and some records to his home. Afterwards, the two of them sat in the kitchen drinking coffee and talking about football. Midnight passed, but still they sat on. Then, suddenly at about two o'clock, John produced a Bible and began to talk about Jesus Christ!

Feeling that he had been tricked into this situation, Patrick became argumentative, and started to disagree with everything his friend said.

But John then told a story about two friends who were walking along a busy road. One of them was aware of the danger of oncoming traffic, but to his horror sees his friend start to cross the road. He pushes the other lad out of the way, and in doing so is killed himself. 'What would you do? asked John, 'if you were the chap who was spared and your friend got killed?'

After a moment's thought, Patrick said 'I would go to my dead friend's parents. I would thank them that their son gave his life saving mine. I would try to be a son to them . . .'. John then asked him if he had ever said Thank You to his heavenly Father for sending His Son to die in his place? He began to show his friend from the Bible that he needed to confess his sin and thank God for sending His Son to be his Lord and Saviour. The Holy Spirit was at work in that kitchen as the two boys talked together. Soon they were kneeling together, and Patrick was committing his life to Jesus Christ.

When Patrick told his mother that something wonderful had happened to him, she thought he had 'won the bingo'. But when he explained that he had made a commitment to Jesus Christ she said: 'Don't worry, son – it'll only be a nine-day wonder!'

But Patrick's conversion was to be no nine-day wonder. His life had been completely turned around. The Biggles books were replaced by such works as Wesley's Sermons and Readings from C. H. Spurgeon. Workmates and family alike were all amazed at the change which had taken place, and although to begin with there were cries of 'Holy Joe' etc., it soon became an accepted thing that Patrick was 'different' – and they respected him for it. When he was called up to do National service, he decided to do three years in the Royal Air Force, where once again his faith was tested.

He began to seek a deeper experience, and to look to God for guidance about the rest of his life. He describes the day when he was 'filled with the holy Spirit', having prayed and longed for this blessing during many days. 'Quite suddenly my heart was filled with a deep sense of the presence of the Lord', he says 'My heart filled with a joy I could not contain. I was filled with an assurance that Jesus Christ was alive – alive in me. It was as if a veil had been lifted from my mind, heart and spirit, and I wept for joy. Jesus had manifested Himself to me and in me. I had tasted the joy unspeakable and full of glory'.

Meanwhile, the mission hall where Patrick worshipped had now appointed a full-time pastor, who encouraged the young people in his care to share the gospel with others. It was he who first sowed the seeds of missionary vision in Patrick's heart. The pastor's method of training bore fruit. When he eventually applied to a Missionary Training College, he had already seen people come to Christ through his preaching and personal witnessing.

'I had even seen my mother weeping in the congregation as I preached the gospel', he says, 'and one of my sisters eventually became a Sunday School teacher.' He began to pray earnestly about his future, promising the Lord he would 'go anywhere and do anything for Him'. He began to enquire how he should go about becoming a missionary, and was recommended to apply to the Worldwide Evangelization Crusade missionary training college in Glasgow. So it came about that two weeks after being de-mobbed from the RAF he arrived on the doorstep of that college to start a two-year course there.

Patrick expresses his sense of fulfilment and promise in his first letter to his friends back home:

'I do thank you for your prayers. It's a real joy to be here. There is so much to praise the Lord for. The study of God's Word is a real joy, and we have so much time for study. The fellowship is just grand. We sing while peeling potatoes, cleaning windows and travelling on the tube around Glasgow! . . .'

By the time he left College, Patrick knew where he should serve as a missionary. He says that as he prayed one day, the land of Japan came into his mind, and he simply told the Lord that if He wanted him there, he would go! And as soon as he did this he experienced a deep sense of peace in his heart.

The college although a place of joy and faith, was also a place of strict discipline, especially in connection with personal relationships. Contact between male and female students was not encouraged, and this suited Patrick fine, he says, to begin with. But there came a time when he began to find it difficult to concentrate during prayer times because the thought of a certain very attractive Scottish student persisted in coming into his mind. He struggled with this for months, until one day it dawned on him that maybe the Lord was trying to tell him something.

Sarah, meantime, was also feeling attracted to Patrick, and both were praying for guidance in the matter. Four years later, they were married in a little Japanese church in the suburbs of Tokyo, for Sarah had also entered College with her heart set on Japan. They were to serve the Lord for thirty years there.

Patrick later wrote a book about his years in Japan, and called it *On Giants Shoulders.*

It is a book written with honesty and sincerity, and has been a blessing to many. It tells the story of a man who had the courage to obey the call of God, with all that such a call entailed. It is the story of a life dedicated to communicating the gospel message – the same message which had transformed him and set him free from the shackles of the past. Above all it is a story which proclaims the greatness of God, and the saving power of His Son Jesus Christ.

When Patrick left College, it was necessary to find out whether he was likely to be able to tackle the difficult Japanese language with any possibility of success, so he was sent to the School of Oriental and African Studies at London university to sit a language aptitude test. He confesses that he was quite overwhelmed by the occasion, and felt totally out of place. At the end of a gruelling day of tests and exercises, he came away feeling despondent and discouraged. But after a six weeks' basic linguistics course with Wycliffe Bible Translators his whole outlook toward language study changed, and he was no longer afraid of the Japanese language.

Hearing Patrick speaking fluent Japanese now, it's hard to believe that he struggled so hard with it in the beginning, but his studies had to continue in language school when he arrived in Japan. Sarah followed him a year later, and was immediately dispatched to Kyoto, where she too studied Japanese while working in the Christian Literature Crusade bookshop, and living in flat above the premises. When she had completed her two years of language study, she and Patrick were married. They were now ready to begin their life of service together.

During the following thirty years they worked among the Japanese people, spreading the gospel message wherever opportunity arose, and ministering to small groups of Christians and seekers. They eventually had three daughters, and took upon themselves the difficult task of educating them at home. Patrick's book is full of fascinating stories about their experiences in Japan and the way that God opened up all kinds of opportunities for them. It tells, too, with moving honesty, of the trials and setbacks which inevitably become part of every life of service.

Patrick was later much in demand by local educationalists, who heard about his emphasis on family life and unity. He was invited to address large gatherings of people at PTA meetings, and his reputation for holding his audiences enthralled increased. One primary school teacher later wrote him a deeply appreciative letter in which he says:

'Your lecture was very clear, understandable, attractive and convincing, as it was told through your experience. It moved us deeply. I was overwhelmed thereby. The only thing I can do is to reflect upon my way of life. I must ask myself if I am living life with such responsibility and consideration as you are. I am sorry to say, No, I am not!'

At one such meeting a publisher was present, and he suggested that the whole series of messages be made into a book. So it came about that *Love Between Parents – A Key to our Children's Future* was published and became a popular evangelistic tool all over Japan. Soon, after each PTA lecture a bookstall was set up, and the people at the lecture bought this book – through which they also learned the Biblical background to the lecture!

At the same time as all this activity, Patrick was continuing his own studies as an external student of London University. He now proceeded to postgraduate studies, and chose as his subject the poetry of one of Japan's most popular poets. Something about this poetry appealed to Patrick, as it seemed to have a touch of the Cockney about it. Consequently he chose the life and work of this poet as a subject for a thesis.

A photograph showing Patrick in his academic robes shortly after graduating as a PhD seems to me to sum up the fascinating story of an East End boy who was called of God to a life of amazing diversity and unstinting service – a life which demonstrates the power of God to transform even the most unpromising material into a force for good in the world.

BRIEF ENCOUNTERS

'To travel pleasantly', it has been said, 'is better than to arrive'. But this may well depend upon the mode of transport you choose. For a number of reasons, my firm favourite still tends to be the railway Since I usually travel mid-morning, early afternoon or late evening, there is usually no problem about getting a seat. In fact, there have been times when I have had a whole carriage to myself for most of the journey.

As I settle back in my seat and get out my book or my newspaper, a comforting sense of isolation seems to wrap itself around me. As the train slides through our beautiful English countryside, running along the bottom of people's gardens, over rivers and around woodland and pastures, I find the whole experience conducive to prayer and praise, and any problems or anxiety I might have seem to melt away.

I have to admit that, though I admire those zealous and courageous souls who aim to start up conversations with a view to evangelising their fellow passengers, I cannot count myself among their number. I so much value the privacy and isolation afforded by the journey, that I almost resent it if someone breaks the sound barrier by trying to engage me in conversation. For once even a few casual words have been spoken between strangers in close proximity, the spell is broken, and it's no longer possible to maintain that closed-in, invisible feeling which, for me, at least, is so precious

Having said all this, I do, as in all walks of life, try to be ready to respond to the person in real need, who might, after all, have been put in my path for that very purpose. I have had one or two odd but significant experiences of this kind, and though I never knew the outcome of the conversations which took place, each one seemed, in its way, to be inevitable.

I was once sitting in the corner of a station waiting room when I felt the eyes of a man nearby fixed broodingly on me. Being past the age for receiving the 'glad eye' from members of the opposite sex, I ventured to look up and see what kind of man it was who was scrutinising me so closely. I saw a nervous-looking individual, about the same age as myself, who, as soon as our eyes met, got up from his seat and came over to where I was sitting.

'I do apologize for bothering you', he said. 'But would you do something for me?' While I hesitated, he went on: 'If you're going on the same train as me, will you help me on to it, and then let me sit with you?'

Alarm bells started to ring, but then he went on: 'I know it's a funny thing to ask, but I just felt you wouldn't mind somehow. You see, I'm recovering from a nervous illness which has left me with a dread of trains. I happened to be travelling on one when my original breakdown happened. And since then, although I'm OK now in every other way, I have this phobia . . . I felt you'd understand somehow. I really do hope you don't mind . . .'

As it happened – (if it did just 'happen') – I did understand, having fairly recently been involved with a person suffering from similar problems. I was not, in fact, going on the same train as this man, but I used the rest of the time at my disposal to encourage him to talk about his breakdown. He then opened up to me about family circumstances which had clearly played a major part in what had happened. I told him how my own faith in God had helped me through difficult times of my own. He said that he did believe, in a way, though there was a lot he did not understand. There was a Baptist Church near where he lived, he said, but he had never actually been inside.

Once more it 'so happened' that I knew the pastor of that Church, and I promised to contact him about my fellow traveller as soon as I returned home, which I duly did. Whatever the outcome of that encounter was, it seemed at the time, important that it should take place.

On another occasion, I was reading a book about loneliness by Martin Israel called *Living Alone*. As the young ticket collector came along to clip my ticket, he caught sight of the book, which I had placed face-downward on my lap while I groped for my ticket. He then took me completely by surprise by saying:

'There's a lot of that about these days!' Puzzled, I asked, 'A lot of what?'

'Loneliness', he said, nodding his head in the direction of my book.

'You're right about that', I said, and as he seemed in no hurry to pass on, I asked him if he lived on his own.

'No', he said. 'Far from it. But you don't have to live on your own to be lonely do you? I've come to the conclusion that some of the loneliest people are those who live in a crowd. It's something deep inside you, isn't it. Hasn't got much to do with people, really, it seems to me.' And with a wistful smile he moved on down the carriage to get on with his job.

When he'd gone, I started to wonder if I should have said more. Then I remembered that I had in my bag a few copies of one of my own books, the first chapter of which deals with loneliness. So I prayed that if I was to give the guard a copy of my book that I would see him again before I left the train. Sure enough, as I got out later on I caught sight of him standing in the doorway a few carriages along. Quickly, I walked along the platform and gave him the book, in which I had already written an inscription.

'Present for you', I smiled as I made for the station exit. I never knew the outcome of that encounter either!

A third happening took place while I was reading another book by the same author. This time entitled *Coming in Glory*. The person concerned was a middle-aged lady who later turned out to be a West End actress on her way to visit friends in London. Leaning forward in her furs and immaculate make-up, she said: 'Pardon me, but are you a Theosophist?'

I must confess I didn't know a lot about Theosophists, but at least I knew I wasn't one! I told her that I was, in fact, on my way to speak to a Women's Coffee Morning, and she wanted to know what my subject would be. This gave me a fine opportunity to share a little of my faith with her. She wished me well as I left her, and her eyes seemed to show that I had left her with something to think about!

Brief encounters . . . ships that pass in the night! (Or should I say 'trains'?) But who knows what joyful and surprising encounters we shall all make when we arrive at our final destination!

ANNE MARIE'S STORY

Anne Marie is a member of our church family who has a moving story to tell. She has written it down, and I have her permission to share it with you:

I suppose it's true to say that my childhood did not really have the best of starts. My dad died of pneumonia when I was two, and my mother, who wasn't really mentally stable, began to get steadily worse. A year later, after a house-fire and various visits from the social services, my younger brother and I were taken to live with our grandparents.

My family were never really what you would call religious, but when you are a child, you never question the existence of God. He's always there, and He's watching you. It never occurs to you that it could be any other way. In my case, this was all suddenly to change. My mother finally committed suicide and died the day after my seventh birthday.

I remember writing a short prayer for every day, but I just felt emptier and emptier as I prayed the prayers. When I got to Wednesday, I'd had enough. I'd asked God to make my mother the brightest star in the sky, but as I looked out of the window, all the stars looked the same – small and alone in a big empty sky. And that is exactly how I felt. I lost my faith that night. I screwed up the piece of paper and threw it into the bin. God wasn't there, and I was alone. I'd have to look after myself from now on, because I was the only one I could rely on. The local Anglican priest, Father David, came around a few times and tried to convince me that God would be there, but in my heart it seemed that I knew better. I sat on the couch and watched cartoons as he talked to me, and blocked him and God out of my head and out of my life.

When I was nine, Father David came to my school and asked for volunteers to start a youth choir at the church. I loved singing, and so I went along. The church was cold and draughty, and had scary statues, but the choir mistress was nice, so I kept going. It was something to do, and it gave me a measure of satisfaction. But when I was eleven, my Granddad died of cancer. He was there one day, and gone the next. All the older ladies at church fussed me and told me I'd meet him again in heaven. I was smiling on the outside, but my heart was dying inside. I was convinced there was no heaven, or God, and if there was, why did He have to take everyone I loved away from me?

A year later, when I was twelve, the priest insisted that I got baptized and confirmed to stay in the choir. So I did. I wore nice clothes, said verses, took the bread and wine and went home. I just went through the motions, felt nothing apart from emptiness and continued at the church choir until I was fifteen. Then one day I realized that I was being hypocritical. I decided to leave, and I never looked back.

Time went by, and I concentrated hard on my studies, because the busier I was, the less everything hurt. Then I started college, and became friendly with a girl who began to talk to me about her faith. I was completely taken aback by her commitment to God, and felt compelled to find out more. I had so many conversations about life in general with her on the college bus, I just couldn't get enough. I was fascinated with everything she said. She made me think that perhaps I had missed something vital somewhere. Perhaps there was something out there, bigger than me, bigger than everything.

Then one night I woke up in the dark and was terrified. I'd never felt anything like it before. I just felt that there was something terribly wrong – something evil in my room. I couldn't move. It was as though a huge weight was bearing down on my chest. I don't know why I did it, but I found myself saying the Lord's Prayer, and really meaning it. I was suddenly filled with an immense warmth. A feeling of well-being and love washed over me like a wave, and in that one moment I felt as if I was being embraced with such love that my heart would break!

In that flood of emotion I knew instantly that God was real. He was there, and He was looking after me. And He loved me!

However, it took another two years for me to come to a full understanding of my faith. When I went to university, God really took hold of my life with both hands. I was standing outside a lecture room on my own and this random girl came up to me and said:

'You're a Guide, aren't you?'

I looked at her as if she was insane.

'Yes', I ventured.

'I've seen you around Hall, and I'm in this lecture too. I needed a conversation starter, and I saw your badge. I'm Josie.'

And that was it. We were inseparable after that. Josie was the most important thing that happened to me in my first year. She introduced me to a wonderful church which was eventually to become my spiritual home. At first I was really sceptical about everything. I understood and believed in God, but just could not get my head around the whole concept of Jesus. I just did not comprehend how such a wonderful man could give up His life to save the very people who crucified Him. I could feel something moving inside me, but I was afraid, and tried to ignore it.

I thought about God, Jesus and the universe over the next year, and finally started to go to church with the others every week. There came a day which turned out to be the greatest day of my life. I don't even remember the service, but remember standing next to my friends and thinking:

'I suddenly understand Jesus' sacrifice! I want Him in my life!'

It was as if a veil had been lifted from my eyes and I was filled with the Holy Spirit. I felt as though Jesus was standing by me holding my hand. I know now that He always had been there. I just wasn't looking before. Since that day my faith has grown so quickly that I feel like a completely different person. It has not always been easy. I have met with opposition from people who simply do not understand. I just cannot believe I went on for so long without God. But I am a new person now. I can share my problems and my love of God more openly. I no longer feel empty and alone. God has filled that void in my soul with His incomparable love. And the community at my church has provided me with so much love, too. I used to walk through the world and feel nothing. There was just me and nothing more. Now I see a world in which God moves in everything. He is everywhere and in everything, and I know that wherever I am, I'll never again be totally alone. Because I belong to Him.

WENDY'S STORY

Wendy was brought out of a life of spiritual darkness and emotional pain through a series of events involving Christians from very different backgrounds. This seems to prove effectively that 'the wind of the Spirit' blows through all our artificial barriers of dogma and tradition.

When she was three years old, Wendy was placed in a children's home. After a while, she was taken into a foster home, and finally adopted. Her adoptive parents knew very little about her background, except that her mother had been unable to cope with her own tangled life, and was quite willing for her child to be adopted. Much later, Wendy was to discover numerous half-brothers and sisters And it was through one of these that she learned of the shocking conditions in which they had lived, before they, too, were abandoned by their mother.

But as a newly adopted child, Wendy was happy and secure. She had a good education at a convent school, though her adoptive parents had no particular church affiliations. But from the age of thirteen, she had puzzled her parents by her strange behaviour. She was in the habit of inflicting damage on herself, tearing at her finger nails, and pricking her gums. Wendy herself did not know why she did these things. But she was vaguely aware of a longing to be free from some unseen enemy, and a terrible sense of rage and fear often threatened to overwhelm her.

Later she became pregnant, and had to move out of the home she had come to know and love. She later married the father of her baby, and set up house with her new young husband. Sadly, when her little boy was born, he lived only for one hour. Wendy was heartbroken.

After the death of her baby, her sense of insecurity increased, and she longed for peace of mind and a freedom from mental pain. Materially, Wendy and her husband prospered. Three daughters were eventually born to them; they enjoyed large houses and cars, with exciting holidays, and all that money could buy. But Wendy was becoming more and more depressed, and began to depend on drink to help blot out her past and her sense of despair.

One day she felt that she had come to the end of hope. She remembers sinking to the floor and pleading with God – if He existed – to help her. It was a genuine cry from the heart. Suddenly, as she sat there on the floor in her comfortable house, she was aware of a living presence entering the room. She knew, without doubt, that God had come to her and put His arms around her. Her cry for help was answered, and she surrendered her life to Him. She was never to be the same again. Her journey of healing was about to begin, though it was to be a painful journey nevertheless.

A year later, after battling unsuccessfully with her old enemy, depression, Wendy had a breakdown, and entered a psychiatric clinic. Now the memories which had been locked away inside her for so long began to be loosened, yet true freedom still eluded her. Hypnotherapy and psychotherapy were tried without success. It was not until someone introduced her to some Christians who recommended a special kind of ministry that the horror of her early life was exposed.

Wendy's mother had been involved in Satanism and witchcraft, and as a tiny child she had been taken along to these gatherings and been subjected to unspeakable horrors. She was systematically tortured and abused emotionally, physically and sexually. As she re-lived the full horror of these events, she needed all the protection that prayer and ministry could bring her. But at long last, she was free.

Now she understood why she had been through such dark days, and why she felt so full of self-hatred and loathing. Her church contacts were mostly Catholic and Anglican, and they had all been praying for her. But Wendy now felt under a compulsion to be baptised by immersion. An overwhelming conviction that this was what she had to do finally led her to seek out Baptist friends, and on a shining Easter Sunday she was finally baptised in the way she deeply desired. It was from this Baptist church that she later received loving care as well as a Bible-based ministry. She would always be grateful for that.

Her baptism was a truly joyous occasion, and as Wendy stood up to give her testimony and tell her story, she paid tribute to all the people who had been instrumental in bringing her to this point. They, along with her three daughters, were all there to rejoice and give thanks with her.

There is an interesting rider to this story. For in spite of much prayer on Wendy's part, her marriage had sadly come to an end. But when she married again, it was to an ex-Catholic priest, and after their wedding, a service of blessing was held in an evangelical Anglican church.

Wendy went on to rejoice in her new-found freedom, realizing that her emotional healing would need to be a continuing process. She recognized her need to walk in her God-given freedom, keeping close to her Lord, and feeding on His Word. Those deeply etched wounds, reaching right back into her childhood, would take time to heal completely.

But this story reminds us that God is able to do 'exceeding abundantly above all that we can ask or even think – according to the power at work within us.' What is more, He can and does, work through all kinds of people and situations to fulfil His purposes in His children. He is not bound by human demarcations. He cuts across them all, and no-one can stand in His way. 'He is mighty to the pulling down of strongholds, and He sets the prisoner free.'

LEARNING TO FORGIVE

'Is there, for men without God, some kind of grace which can cure hatred and resentment? Or must these deep, fatal traces remain forever unredeemed?'

Thus ran the blurb on the dust cover of a novel which tells the story of a man looking back over his childhood and seeing only delinquency and moral disaster. Brought up in an orphanage where a distorted view of Christianity was presented to him at a time when he needed care and understanding, he reviews the negative emotions which have shaped his destiny. He thinks of the chain reaction of deprivation, pain, resentment, anger, and finally hatred – and feels himself to be lost.

I was reminded of an interview I watched on television between Mavis Nicholson and another well know novelist. The writer spoke of her own childhood, when both she and her brother had been sexually abused by their father, and how they had carried a burden of resentment and hatred with them all through their lives. Then one day, when she was shopping in the supermarket, she suddenly stopped dead in her tracks and said aloud: 'But I loved the old man! In spite of everything, I loved him!' From that day on, she said, she was liberated, set free from what had become an intolerable burden. Yet for her brother, no such miracle had yet occurred, and he remained as bitter as ever.

I found this admission of love for a parent who had deeply wronged and damaged his daughter profoundly moving, especially since she made no claim to religious belief of any kind. Somehow it offends our tidy, orthodox minds to have to concede that the same healing grace can be as available to the non-believer as it is the believer. I love the honesty of Corrie Ten Boom in her book *Tramp for the Lord.* The story of how she did battle with intensely hostile feelings when asked to shake hands with a converted Nazi guard from the notorious Ravensbruck concentration camp where she and her family had been so cruelly treated is now a classic one.

Her sister had died in the camp, and Corrie had witnessed unspeakable cruelties which remained etched on her mind for years. So later, when she had been addressing a large meeting in Germany, and this tall familiar figure approached her from the back of the hall, she could not at first believe her eyes. And then she recognised him. It was one of the most hated guards from the concentration camp. Bewildered, she heard him tell her how he had found Christ since the ending of the awful regime, and wanted to make amends in any way he could. Begging her forgiveness, he held out his hand for Corrie to shake.

Everything within her cried out against the enormity of what he was asking, and all the old painful images flashed before her eyes. 'I felt I could not forgive. It was too much to ask. I could not take that hand, the hand which had inflicted so much cruelty upon innocent people – upon my own dear family.' Then she remembered that Jesus had forgiven her. That He had forgiven the soldiers who nailed Him to the cross. And she prayed that God would make it possible for her to do the same.

It was then that she felt the love of Christ flooding her heart. She reached out and took that man's hand in her own, and immediately felt her heart to be set free from bitterness. It was a lesson she was never to forget. Later, she set up a home in Holland for victims of

Nazi brutality. And here she saw an interesting principle at work.

'Those who were able to forgive their former enemies were able to return to the outside world and rebuild their lives, no matter what the physical scars. Those who nursed their bitterness remained invalids. It was as simple and as horrible as that.'

There is considerable evidence that negative feelings, if allowed to grow and take root, can affect not only our minds and our personalities, but our physical health. The body will react with all kinds of disabling symptoms when wrong attitudes – no matter how well justified – are allowed to gain control of us. Some people find that they have to do battle with these 'deep, fatal traces, for the rest of their lives'. Corrie Ten Boom has said, with endearing honesty, that she wishes she could say that merciful and charitable thoughts just naturally flow from her to others since her encounter with the former Nazi guard. But they don't, she says.

She thought forgiving Christian friends who had wronged her would be child's play. It wasn't! When some people she loved and trusted did something which hurt her, she seethed inside for weeks, until at last she asked God to work His miracle in her as He had done before. He did, and she was restored to peace of mind once more. Then suddenly, in the middle of the night, she woke up and started rehashing the whole affair again. Finally, she sat in bed and asked God to help her not only forgive, but to forget.

What a comfort such honest admissions of failure are! We recognise ourselves in these stories of human frailty. Corrie actually goes on to say that she learned another secret about forgiveness through this episode. It is not enough to simply say, 'I forgive you'. The forgiveness must be lived out in practical ways, and this can be very hard to do. In this instance, she went on to burn some of the letters which had been carefully preserved as evidence of wrong-doing.

For the Christian, it should surely be less difficult to forgive than for the non-believer, since the teachings of Jesus on the subject are so clear and familiar to us. But Paul told us to 'beware, lest any of you fail of the grace of God', allowing 'a root of bitterness to spring up' and trouble not only us, but many others around us. The bitterness that erupts in some folk as they speak of the wrongs done to them in the past, can be really ugly to behold, and can make the listener recoil as though some of the venom has touched him or her personally.

I have heard the three words 'I hate him' spoken with such ferocity that the face of the speaker has been distorted. Sometimes there is no question of an 'admission' as such. The statement has come out more as a triumphant declaration. At such times it is not easy to suggest that Christ's forgiveness is as valid for the person who has perpetrated the wrong as it is for the sufferer.

'Forgiveness' says Corrie, 'is the key which unlocks the door of resentment, and the handcuffs of hatred'.

WHEN LOVE BREAKS THROUGH

When Anne, a retired music teacher, read a newspaper article about an organisation which puts death-row prisoners in touch with people in the outside world, she decided to reply.

On the other side of the Atlantic, in Florida State prison, Roy had already spent thirteen years in a cell next door to the electric chair. He had been involved in a kidnap robbery that ended in murder. But due to the fact there was an element of doubt about whose finger had been on the trigger of the gun, appeal procedures had been put into motion. During his long period of waiting for the final death sentence to be passed, four death warrants had been issued and then temporarily rescinded.

Anne, writing from the tranquillity of her country home, little knew that her simple step of replying to the newspaper article would lead her up a path of strange joy and sorrow. At the time, the reason she gave for embarking on such a venture was that it was 'something she felt she could do'. She liked writing letters, and she had time to spare.

The story of the brief but intense friendship that developed between Anne and Roy is movingly beautiful. At first their letters were naturally cautious and restrained, although from the outset Roy made no attempt to hide his delight in the fact that someone had cared enough to write to a stranger in a far country.

The arrival of the blue and white airmail letters became the highlight of Roy's day. He replied promptly to each letter, telling her about the daily routine of prison life, about the ever present threat of the electric chair, abut the added torture of uncertainty. But he wrote with dignity, and a kind of resignation which touched Anne's heart.

Photographs were exchanged, and then, gradually, the tone of the letters deepened, as each shared feelings which had been opened up by what the other had written. Anne found herself drawn into the silent suffering of this man not quite young enough to be her son. She longed to be able to alleviate his pain in any way she could. She tactfully enquired whether one was allowed to send books or money for every day comforts.

But Roy assured her that the greatest comfort of all for him came from reading her letters. He had placed her photograph on his locker, and would gaze at it as he read the letters. Anne, on holiday in the Yorkshire Dales with her husband, wrote of the beauty of the hills and the open countryside, and of her longing to share it in some small way with Roy. Gradually she found herself being involved more deeply and emotionally with his plight. Her heart ached for him, and her concern showed through the words that she wrote.

Roy, in turn, began to open up his heart to her. He told her how he had once fathered a son whom he had never seen. Writing to Anne, he said, had opened up emotions which had been locked away inside him for years. Now he was concerned that when his execution should finally take place, that his new friend would be upset. It saddened him to think of the pain he would have brought her. As he began to allow himself to feel again, all kinds of buried instincts began to emerge.

As for Anne, she was moved to tears by what Roy had written. That a man in his position should be concerned for her in this way was a development of such significance that she was stirred to the very depths of her being. She wrote and told him so, in her quiet, unpretentious way of using words which somehow conveyed the gentleness of her caring disposition.

Then one day, the news came that the judicial appeals had failed, and the date of the execution was imminent. Roy was to go to the electric chair. Distraught, Anne did everything that she could to relieve Roy's suffering, oblivious of the fact that her own pain was by now as deep as his. She wrote that she did not believe death was the end of the road for anyone. She believed in God, she said, and could not accept that this life, with all its confusion and sadness, could possibly be all that there was for us.

Anne's husband, concerned for his wife, and anxious to do what he could, 'phoned the authorities in the State prison. Permission was given for Anne to speak to Roy for five minutes. She told him beforehand that he would have to do most of the talking, as she feared she would be struck dumb with emotion when she heard his voice. But the conversation they had was quietly intimate, as their letters had finally been.

'I want you to know' he wrote later, just before he went to his death, 'that the last living image in my mind was your dear, sweet face. Pray for me if you like.'

Later, Anne discovered that Roy had been the victim of a very traumatic childhood, and had been finally turned out on to the streets by drunken parents. She was shown a photograph of a wide-eyed little boy, clutching a teddy bear, and of a dark young man with haunted eyes. The picture of the forty-nine-year-old who finally went to the electric chair was of a strong, handsome man: a man who knew, at last, what it meant to be loved.

Back in England, Anne was devastated by Roy's death, as she knew she would be. Her family had been supremely supportive during the period of her correspondence with the condemned man.

But if they felt secretly relieved that the episode was over and the task completed, their relief would have been short-lived. For Anne later offered herself to correspond with yet another death-row prisoner. No doubt she knew now with a deep certainty, the supreme value of what had been wrought through her correspondence with Roy. For, paradoxically, she had provided a dying man with a lifeline.

ALL AT SEA

Shock waves reverberated around certain sections of the Church when it was reported that a vicar had written a book saying he did not believe in God. The sense of outrage which followed this report was graphically portrayed in a cartoon which appeared next day in one of the national newspapers. It showed a butchers' shop displaying a placard stating that the proprietors, though still continuing with their business, had become vegetarians!

The book in question apparently set out to explain that the author could no longer accept the idea of a God who intervened in human affairs. But despite the fact that he had felt compelled to forsake the orthodox doctrines of the Church, he did not see why he could not carry on his work as a parish priest.

As is usually the case in such matters, people tended to take sides, and a number of folk declared their intention of staying loyally by their vicar in spite of public opinion that he should go.

At about the same time as this book was published, I happened to tune in to a television programme where a seaman from the northern seaside town of Scarborough was being interviewed. He had an extraordinary story to tell. He described how one day during a storm at sea he had been swept into the hold of his boat by a strong wind which slammed the hatchway down upon his arm as he fell As he lay in agony, his arm damaged, darkness surrounding him, unable to move, he was aware of a feeling of utter helplessness – helplessness and despair.

All his life he had been a hard drinking man, given to bad language, and having no time for people who believed in God. He declared himself to be an atheist, and lived his life accordingly. But in that moment of crisis, something happened to him which he later found hard to explain, or even to put into words. He had become suddenly aware that someone was lifting him up out of the darkness and bringing him out of the hold of the boat. What is more, he knew without any doubt that the 'someone' was God.

'I could never have lifted that hatchway up', he said. 'My damaged arm was useless, and I was barely conscious.'

But now, as he found himself safely back on the deck of the ship, blinking in the bright sunlight, he knew that God had delivered him not only from the darkness of the hold, but from the darkness of sin and unbelief. God had broken into his life without even being invited., and from that time on, he says, he was a changed man. No more drunkenness and swearing, he said. He knew himself to be a Christian and was proud of it.

Why did God intervene in the life of that Scarborough seaman? Was there, underneath the hard exterior of this man, a deeply unconscious yearning, a kind of secret reaching out for God. Who can tell? But one thing is certain: the conversion of this man could not have come about without the divine intervention of a God of love who is ready to answer even before we call.

No book, no matter how sincere and scholarly its author, and no matter how genuinely researched and put together, can stand against the testimony of such a man as that seaman, and millions of others like him – lives which have been transformed by the invading love of God.

What does it take to convince a sceptic of the existence of God, and of the truth of the gospel message? I would suggest that the most convincing proof of all lies in the almost unconscious witness of those who, against all odds, have displayed this truth in their lives. At the service of thanksgiving held for the release of Terry Waite and the other hostages, the vicar said a very significant thing:

'To those who say, How can there be a God? I would reply: How can there not be a God when such men as these, having survived years of mistreatment, isolation and darkness, come back to us strong and radiant with their faith in God deepened, and with no trace of bitterness in their hearts. How else can such a miracle be explained?'

And surely the precious jewel at the heart of our faith is the God-given ability to forgive. Jesus, on that first historic Good Friday cried: 'Father, forgive them' . . . as the cruel nails were driven into His flesh. It is because He lives in them that so many of His followers have been able to echo those words all down the ages. In the face of such a clearly divine quality, the unbeliever must surely be stunned into silence.

How could the father of a beloved daughter killed by the IRA declare, and go on declaring, that he forgave her murderers. And how could the wife whose husband had been in a coma for nearly three years speak only of the joy of being able to take him home – even though he is never likely to regain consciousness? Where is the bitterness one would expect – where the hatred?

How could Jean Wadell, when questioned on TV, turn our minds from her own sufferings to the suffering of her ruthless captors? That, said the interviewer, visibly shocked, is a supremely Christian thing to say. And when Terry Anderson was asked what was the worst thing his captors did to him he replied: 'They made my loved ones suffer – that is worst thing they did. But do I hate them? As a Christian, I forgive – I have to forgive, for that is the Christian way!'

The same light that glowed in the face of the risen Saviour on that first Easter morning transforms the faces of these modern-day saints as they speak. No wonder the Psalmist said that only a fool can really believe there is no God!

A BOWL OF CHERRIES

One of the most moving stories to come out of the hostage release drama was one told by John MacCarthy not long after his return to this country. After years of isolation and poor diet, there came a time when a small group of men found themselves together in one cell. Into their grey and black world one day came one of the guards carrying a bowl of cherries.

John MacCarthy described how the sheer beauty of this simple dish of glowing fruit made such an impact on the men – starved as they were of all visual enjoyment – that they sat for a whole day just looking at the bowl of cherries before finally eating and enjoying them.

During his debriefing, MacCarthy also found that his attention could be totally diverted from any matter in hand if, for example, a rose in a nearby vase should catch his eye. So deep was his need to feast his eyes on the rose, that he became totally absorbed by it to the exclusion of all else. The human spirit, when denied the natural beauties of life which we all take for granted, clearly craves them as the starved body craves food.

When asked about his ill-treatment at the hands of his captors, John refused to be drawn into discussion. Putting it all to one side, he emphasized his wish to forget what had happened in those early years, and to concentrate on the good and positive side of his ordeal. The things uppermost in his mind, he said, were the friendships formed and the lessons learned during his captivity.

Paul's injunction to the Philippians is maybe one of the best pieces of advice we can take to ourselves in times of stress or darkness:

> Whatever is true, whatever is honourable, whatever is just,
> whatever is pure, whatever is lovely, whatever is gracious
> – if there is any excellence, if there is anything worthy of
> praise – think on these things!

There are times when we need to turn our eyes from the vast canvases of world history and concentrate on the small details which could so easily go unnoticed. For it is in the hidden, secret places that God is always at work, bringing into being the kind of victories which, though the world may scoff and deride, are the very stuff of eternity.

A BATTLE WON

A certain Sergeant Major tells of how, on the eve of leading his men into battle during the Gulf War, he sat down to do some serious thinking. He had been impressed by the fact that Christians in the homeland were writing letters to soldiers with the intention of cheering them and reminding them that they were not forgotten. That complete strangers should bother to do such a thing struck this Sergeant Major as being truly remarkable.

When some of the younger men began to come to him and confess that they were fearful of what lay ahead of them, he didn't know what to say. A Sergeant Major did not dare to admit that he, too, was afraid. So he went to the Padre for some advice.

'I'd like to be able to pray for them', he said. 'But I wouldn't know how.'

The Padre pointed out that all he had to do was to go to God and say exactly what was on his heart – just as he was doing now. So the Sergeant Major went away and did just that. He describes how, to begin with, he felt a sense of total unworthiness. He felt that before he started to pray for the men in his care, he should ask forgiveness for himself, for the many times in which he had failed to match up to even his own standards for living.

He then felt as though a great burden was lifted, and though the day of battle was indeed a tough one, so real was the sense of God's presence that the day became a turning point in this man's life. He committed himself to Christ and has never looked back. And who can measure the spiritual fruit of one such encounter with the living God. The faithful intercessors, the writers of encouraging letters, the folk who quietly go about their business, speaking a word in season as the occasion arises, will one day take precedence over kings and rulers and all the big names of human history.

JOHN'S STORY

John walked into our church coffee club one Friday morning, taking us all by surprise. He was unkempt, unshaven, and smelt strongly of drink. Naturally, we made him welcome, gave him coffee, and asked him how he came to hear about the club. He said that he had simply read the sign outside the building, and decided to come in. Although women tend to be in the majority in this group, there are one or two men as well, so John was soon made to feel at home.

Our club is mainly for friendship and various kinds of non-demanding activities. Although we are attached to a Baptist Church, and run by several of its members, we do not introduce religious subjects, or try to encourage people to come to church. However, John made it fairly clear from the beginning that he had no interest in church or religion of any kind – and that he was, in fact an atheist. But when he had been coming along for several weeks, he began to open up to some of us, telling us a little about his life.

He was obviously a well-read, intelligent man, and prided himself on his various areas of knowledge. We noticed that, as the weeks went by and John had become a regular visitor at the club, his appearance began to change. He began to shave regularly, had obviously bought himself some new clothes, and looked altogether more presentable. He was still drinking and smoking quite heavily, and admitted that he would be in a better state of health if he could cut some of these things out. But he wanted us all to know just how much our friendship and warmth made to him. On the day that he stood up and said this publicly, we were naturally very moved. After all, this is what our club was all about.

As Christmas approached, and we all started to think about sending cards, John informed us that he did not send or receive any cards at Christmas. He then revealed to some of us that he was completely out of touch with his family. After his divorce, and the acrimony which followed it, his three daughters and his sisters had cut themselves off from him, and he did not even know where all of them lived Now, in his late fifties, he was a lonely, and embittered man. Several of us had quietly intimate conversations with him, gently attempting to help him work through his pain. But John made it plain that he did not want that kind of help. Clearly he felt that all the blame for what had gone wrong laid at the door of others, and that there was nothing he could do about that!

There came a time when some of our members heard about Alpha courses, and wanted to join. John was asked if he would be interested, but he emphasized once again that he was an unbeliever, and that nothing whatsoever would change that. If he did go on a course, he declared, he would do so as 'Devil's advocate'. He was told that this would be just fine, as everyone on an Alpha course was encouraged to ask questions, or to talk about their doubts. So he came along, but true to his promise, made things as difficult as possible for the leaders in the process!

Meantime, John's health began to deteriorate, and he was often absent from the club. But he kept in touch, and came along whenever he had a respite from his sickness. Then one day he collapsed, and was taken into hospital suffering from a slight stroke.

It was whilst he was in hospital that he began to do some serious thinking. Having scorned the Bible for so long, he suddenly decided he might as well start reading it to see what it was all about.

Remembering how friends he had met at the club had so often tried to show him how getting to know God could change his life, John said later:

> As I had no close relationship at all at that time, I thought: Well, why not? I could see that the easiest way of doing this was to start by reading the Bible. Though not totally ignorant of the Bible, I had never sat down, read it and studied it word by word. So this is what I did. Not knowing where to start, I decided to start at the beginning – which made absolute sense to me.

John's health, in the meantime began to deteriorate further, and he was diagnosed with cancer. Undeterred, he continued his study of the Bible, and also agreed to allow one of his friends from the club to make contact with one of his sisters. Arrangements were made for this sister to come from her home in Wales and to stay with the club member who had made the contact. From there she visited her brother in hospital, and was reconciled to him – after twelve years of estrangement. During the following weeks and months, all of John's daughters had been traced, and had come to see their father. But now the man they met was a completely different person from the one who had walked away from them all those years ago. John tells how this transformation came about:

'The knowledge of God came to me through the back door, as it were. I was lying one evening in pain, just musing on the serious situation in which found I myself, when I felt a sudden growing sense of warmth and light, a low glow spreading through me from my feet, through my body and heart into my brain. It was similar to the effect one gets when one switches on an electric lamp – you can see the element start to warm up and when it reaches a certain level, it bursts fully into light and gives off maximum heat. This was like a ball in the centre of me. Neither the heat nor the light were like anything I had experienced before.

'When I noted this, I realised that it was the love of God entering my soul very gradually until it burst into a whole, complete feeling Since this happened, I have been praying and talking to God, and all those people who have been urging me to become a Christian have been proven right, I am happy to say! There was one reference in particular which came home to me – one which I had been trying to avoid. I commend it to everyone, already converted or not. It comes from 1 John 1:8-10:

> If we claim to be without sin, we deceive ourselves and the truth is not in us. If we confess our sins, he is faithful and just to forgive us our sins and purify us from all unrighteousness. If we claim we have not sinned, we make him out to be a liar and his word has no place in our lives.

There came a time when John was ready to give his testimony. He did it from his wheelchair in hospital, before an audience of a dozen or more club members. There was hardly a dry eye among them! They had all been praying for John for so long, and one in particular could not help remembering the exact words of the prayer she had said for so many months:

'Please, Lord' she had prayed, 'break into John's unbelief, and fill him with your love and light . . .' And this is exactly what took place!

When John's daughters and sisters were reconciled with him, it was all extremely moving for everybody concerned. They were amazed at the change in him, and so grateful for all that had been done for him by the local Christians. John felt that his experience of conversion had spread ripples which would have far-reaching effects, and that thought brought him great joy. As he apologized to his family for all the hurts, and they in turn asked forgiveness from him, there were some truly precious moments which will never be forgotten.

Before he died, John said that his only regret was for the wasted years. 'I want to use my voice to praise my God now, he said, for as long as I am able.'

AN EXTRAORDINARY LIFE

The name of Patricia St. John may conjure up for some the memory of certain story books, in particular *The Tanglewoods Secret* and *Treasures of the Snow*. These titles, possibly because they were both made into feature films and televised by the BBC might well be the only connection most of us are able to make with the name of this extraordinary woman.

Apart from having written more than twenty books, Patricia spent twenty-seven years of her life as a missionary in Morocco, and for the last ten years of her strenuous, adventure-packed life, was President of Global Care, an international charity which seeks to meet the needs of children in some of the world's poorest countries. When her autobiography was published, many people were amazed to discover all that this remarkable woman had achieved during her lifetime.

Michelle Guinness described Patricia as 'one of the greatest saints I have ever met. Instinctively, in her presence, you knew you were being given a fresh glimpse of the radiance, dignity and graciousness of Christ Himself . . .' Such an accolade might lead one to believe that Patricia was a model of propriety, too good to be true, and probably completely out of touch with reality. Nothing could be further from the truth.

'Patricia, I can see your knickers', called Granny from the bedroom window, as her tomboy granddaughter turned somersaults on the lowest bough of the apple tree. And at school she once climbed out of a skylight window and sat astride the roof reading, while her terrified teachers gathered outside and stared up at her, afraid to call out in case she fell.

When her mother said she had dedicated three of her children to God to serve as missionaries, they accepted the news philosophically, and decided they had better begin a campaign to toughen themselves up. This included sleeping under their beds without covers, walking along the gable roof of the outside toilet, and scratching their arms in order to sign their names in blood! They found a recipe for dandelion wine, and having decided they needed refreshments for their 'club' meetings, proceeded to brew it behind a curtain in their bedroom. The bottles burst loudly all over the room in the middle of the night – and, according to an uncle who tasted what was left in one of the bottles, the children would all have been roaring drunk had they imbibed even one glass each of it!

Their father was away from home more often than not, so much of the upbringing of the five children was left to their mother. One year, when Mr. St. John was to be abroad for a long period, the rest of the family set off to spend the whole period in Switzerland. Here Patricia's inspiration for *Treasures of the Snow* was born. But her account of her actual life at home and at school in that country is a literary gem in itself.

When she was twenty years old, having completed her training as a nurse, she decided to join her brother Farnham, who was working as a missionary doctor in Morocco So the next time he came home, she packed a rucksack and announced that she would ride pillion on his motorbike all the way to North Africa via Europe. They roared off one morning with only the basic requirements on their backs, and arrived in Tangier eight days later, sleeping by the roadside and in ditches, and surviving on slices of sausage and portions of rice.

Patricia describes the hair-raising experience of crossing the border into Spain, and zooming upwards round hairpin bends into the Pyrenees, then zigzagging down to the plains of Madrid and on toward the coast above Gibraltar, before finally crossing by ferry to Tangier.

Working alongside her brother in the hospital at Tangier brought a measure of satisfaction to Patricia, but eventually she felt drawn to the people in the outlying villages. The physical and spiritual need of these Muslim folk – especially the women and children – challenged her at her deepest level, and she finally went to live alone among them for five years.

Her account of these years is full of endearing and amusing stories. Before long, some of the women had come to accept Christianity – largely through Patricia's simple love for them – and her 'wordless' book. This was a set of coloured pages depicting the gospel message in simple terms – black representing sin, blood the death of Christ, gold for salvation, etc. The women's devotion to the Englishwoman, and their newfound freedom, made them anxious to spread the word to their friends and relatives. The simplicity of their faith was often rewarded with amazing answers to prayer, which put even Patricia to shame.

She watched one woman standing over an empty basket, and calling upon God to fill it with much needed wool for their handicrafts. She admits to serious misgivings – but hours later a message came from brother Farnham saying he would be calling next day with a packet of wool which had just arrived from Switzerland. Needless to say, there was much rejoicing among all concerned, not the least in Patricia's heart. For she felt she had so much to learn from these simple folk.

But, inevitably, opposition eventually came to a head in this Muslim society, and Patricia was forbidden by the authorities to teach Christianity to the womenfolk. Any of them who still persisted in following the foreign woman's teaching would be beaten and imprisoned. Reluctantly, Patricia was compelled to depart, leaving a nucleus of strong, secret believers behind to carry on her work, and to mourn her loss.

Throughout all this, Patricia continued to write. She produced three children's novels, a biography of Hudson Taylor, and a book of poetry. After returning to England to nurse her ailing father, of whom she had seen so little as a child, Patricia then returned to Morocco and wrote his biography. Her tribute to him in her autobiography shows how devoted she was to him, bearing him no grudge for his absenteeism during her formative years. She was then asked to write a history of the Rwanda revival, and her exploration of this historic event has some fascinating sidelights and observations to make.

Later, when her mother and Farnham's mother-in-law came out to Tangier to be cared for, Patricia's account of these two saintly old ladies, both bed-ridden and sharing a room together, is most touching. She tells how the presence of God was so real in the room that people loved to come and visit. Bored, rich elderly English ladies, tired of the constant round of cocktail parties, would come and read aloud to them.

'Something happened to me in that room', said one kind society lady after the Grannies died. 'I found a peace I had not known before. I think I came to know God.'

When, eventually, Patricia returned to England, she settled down with her sister Hazel near Coventry. But her missionary heart drew her out time and time again – to Ethiopia, to Bangladesh – wherever there was particular need. She became deeply involved with the plight of the Kurdish refugees after the Gulf War, and then with the needs of children in Romania and Albania, eventually becoming president of Global Care. She undertook arduous travel under nightmare conditions at a time in her life when most people have long retired from active life.

At home, her love for children and young people continued to involve her in all kinds of activities. One evening on her way to church, she passed a group of teenage lads sitting on the steps of the local fish and chip shop. As she passed, they started to sing, in a half-teasing way: 'Grandma, we love you!' – and she turned round to tell them that she loved them, too! 'Can we come round to your house, then?' they called out. So Patricia said that if they cared to go round later, when she came out of church, they'd be welcome.

She arrived home later to find them all on her doorstep. Thus began a weekly get-together in her home for this group of tough youths, who drank tea, listened to her telling Bible stories, and would not go home without their usual goodnight prayer. And all this at the very end of the twentieth century! Throughout her selfless life, she touched thousands with the love of God, and her books have influenced countless people all over the world. She was a truly remarkable woman. And surely a modern-day saint, though she would be the first to deny it, and to give all the honour to God.

A NEW BEGINNING

Some years ago, the novelist Marie Joseph wrote a book about her battle with arthritis. She called it *One Step at a Time*, and it was an inspiration to other sufferers because of Marie's cheerful, uncomplaining attitude toward her condition.

However, there was a time when she went through a period of depression. While this was happening, she felt that the smiling face she presented to the world was actually a mockery of the deep and spiritual trauma through which she was actually passing. At this time, she was writing mainly short stories, but even the motivation to do this dwindled eventually. She felt herself to be slipping into a kind of wilderness where she searched for some nameless source of satisfaction.

'I wanted . . . Oh, I didn't know what I wanted', she wrote. Although she would not have described herself as a religious person, Marie had a vague faith in God. Sometimes she prayed, and occasionally recited Psalm 23 to help her sleep at night. But now, approaching middle age, and haunted by the fear that she might never write again, she began to think back over her life.

Her mother had died giving birth to her, and her father had disappeared soon afterwards. Marie was brought up by her grandmother, and then by an aunt. She often longed to see her father, who she knew was now married to someone else and had children of his own. 'But I was his first baby!' she remembered saying to her grandmother.

She remembered, too, the faith she had known as a child, and as an impressionable adolescent. As a Methodist, she had gone to chapel twice every Sunday, sitting in a hard-backed pew, dressed in the coat kept specially for 'best'. In the afternoons, there would be Sunday School, and the superintendent would talk to the children about the love of God in such a way that they knew it came from his heart.

'Jesus had seemed to be a very real person to me then', she recalled. 'We weren't clever enough to be cynical. Was that why we had such a happy acceptance?' Thinking about it all, she realised that she no longer wanted what she called the trappings of religion – or 'Churchianity' as one friend called it – but the Christianity she'd known as a child.

What she really wanted was something real and personal. In her heart was a kind of wordless cry for help. But now, she thought, she was a grown woman, and her mind was cluttered with the whys and wherefores, and miracles didn't happen – not in this day and age.

The silent cry was still echoing in her heart as the telephone rang. On the line was a publisher who said he wanted to publish the novel she had sent him much earlier, before she went into hospital. She had almost forgotten about it.

This was to be Marie's first published novel, and set her on the road to success. She never forgot how that phone call had seemed to come as an answer to her unspoken need – her silent cry for help.

Time and again one hears of someone who has reached out –no matter how tentatively – toward God in their hour of darkness, and found Him ready and waiting to respond. Sometimes the person concerned has, after an initial upsurge of awe and gratitude, reverted to their previous half-believing, half-doubting state. For others, there is a definite turning point; a conversion from the old life, a spiritual rebirth.

But whatever the outcome, we are left with the humbling knowledge that God, in His graciousness and love, waits constantly for the creatures He brought into being to recognize their need of Him – just as surely as the father in the gospel story waited and watched daily for the return of the prodigal son. We have only to reach out a hand toward Him, and He is already running with both arms outstretched, to meet us.

MARGARET'S STORY

I have known Margaret for quite a number of years and have heard her speak about some of the remarkable things which happened to her when she was a young girl. Now she has given me permission to include part of her story in this book, and I am grateful to her for that, for she has led a truly remarkable life.

Margaret was born in China, as her parents were serving as missionaries there at the time of her birth. Her father actually went out as a single man, but later met the girl who was to become his wife, when she arrived in Chengdu from her home in Canada. Three children were born to them, Margaret being the eldest. This was a time when warlords were fighting to increase their power and to enlarge their territories. As a little girl Margaret remembers hearing conversations about the warlords, but took it all as a matter of course.

Her childhood in China was a happy one. When she was seven years old, she had to go to school. It was impossible to obtain an English education in Chengdu, so she had to go all the way down the Yangtze River by boat to Shanghai. From there she travelled by steamer to Yantai on the Shandong peninsular. Here she joined 300 English and American boys and girls in a school where they were fitted to inhabit the world of their parents' home countries. To be separated from her parents was not an easy thing for Margaret, but every Christmas she made the arduous journey back up the Yangtze River to Sichuan Province.

It was on one of these journeys that Margaret's first adventure began. She was on her way back from Sichuan on board a steamer, heading back to school in Yantai. There were about seventy British schoolchildren all together, and several school teachers. It was winter at the time, and Margaret was eight years old. Soon they left the muddy waters of the Hwang Po estuary and entered the blue waters of the sea. On the boat, the little children had their meals first, and the older people ate later. Margaret remembers that she was drinking soup with an enormous spoon, when suddenly there were sounds of shouts and gunfire. The ship's captain and officers were British. To everyone's horror, one of the officers was shot. Fortunately, he was not killed, but a Russian guard on the ship was. He was later given a burial at sea.

Moments later, the men who were doing the shooting rushed up the stairs to where the children were eating their meal. Now it was clear who they were – Chinese pirates, intent on gaining as much money as they could from the passengers on the boat. The leader was a rough-looking man wearing a purple checked jacket, and all his companions were fiercely following their leader. Everyone put up their hands to stop the shooting, and Margaret remembers putting her small hands up too.

Eventually the pirates realised that there was no money to be had, as those on board were mostly children. What were they going to do with them? They now planned to take over the boat and use it to return to their home, north of Hong Kong. They shut all the cabin windows and guarded all the doors with their guns. The children and their teachers were prisoners. No-one was allowed out on deck.

The pirates then set about disguising the boat by painting the funnel a different colour. They then smashed the radio so there could be no communication with the outside world. The boat should have sailed north to Yantai, but they turned it around and began to sail south. For two whole days they travelled south with all the doors and windows shut, and nobody in the outside world knew that there was anything wrong.

When the boat failed to arrive at its proper destination, the teachers at Yantai became really anxious. What had happened to those seventy children? Where were they? Telegrams were sent to all concerned – the parents and carers – and everyone started praying for the children who had disappeared. It was a terrible time for all concerned. But many of the parents could not be contacted because of communication problems. Margaret's parents were far away in Sichuan, and didn't know anything had happened until it was all over.

But on board the boat, things were happening. On the fourth day of their captivity, the British Royal Air Force was out looking for them. Now the pirates wanted to escape. They began shooting at passing Chinese junks and made them take them to their Bias Bay haunt. At last the children were free. They opened the doors and rushed out onto the deck looking for mementoes of their hair-raising adventure.

When the British captain eventually took the ship into Hong Kong, the children were treated as the little heroes and heroines that they surely were. Later, back at Shanghai, there was tremendous thanksgiving by the parents that these children had been brought safely through their ordeal. They were taken to the Palace Hotel and treated to a party with conjuring tricks and ice cream – a great treat in those days. Soon it was time to go back on board ship for two more days' journey northward. They arrived back at school eventually, and Margaret had her ninth birthday on the day of their arrival.

She tells that even at this young age, she was aware that God was taking care of her. She knew Him to be a 'very present help in times of trouble' and never forgot how she had been kept safe from the pirates, and how all the prayers of God's people had been answered. She was certainly going to need this precious assurance as the years went by. Her teenage years were happy ones, but after Pearl Harbor, in 1941, things changed. This was when Japan joined Germany in fighting the Allies, and suddenly the British and Americans in eastern China became enemies of the Japanese. They were put into internment camps.

At first the children were held as prisoners in their school compound. But later they were moved to a civilian internment camp in Yantai. They were marched from their school to the other end of the city, while their mattresses and baggage came by truck. Then they shut the gates. Margaret, as a young teenager, was in that camp for ten months, along with her brother. The men and boys, though, were in another compound on the hill. They were all made to learn to count in Japanese, so that a double check could be made that no-one had escaped.

Ten months later the Japanese decided to close the camp in Yantai, and make one large camp in Weihsien. The journey to Weihsien was terrible. The prisoners were put into the hold of a boat where they transported grain, produce and merchandise. There was a constant battle with cockroaches, and Margaret was crammed into a small space with three other people for two days and nights. She admits that this was the worst time of her life. But somehow, even in such dire conditions, this young girl was aware that God was her Father, and that He had her in His care. The nightmare boat journey came to an end, and the detainees were put on a train – and finally on trucks – to join others in Weihsien. Together they were 1,400 internees crammed into an American Presbyterian Mission Compound which had been a teaching hospital, a school and a College.

Margaret and her brother were desperately lonely in this camp at first. They had not seen their parents for several years, and although they knew that they were loved, and were being prayed for constantly, life was tough for the two youngsters. They were allowed to send and to receive the occasional letter, but they were permitted to write only twenty-five words. The letter then had to be censored by the Japanese, and only if it was considered suitable would it be sent. Fortunately the Red Cross were responsible for this arrangement, so the lines of communication, though slender, were kept open.

As the war progressed, things got worse. Food became scarce, the young people's clothes wore out, or became too small as they grew. Margaret remembers unpicking a sweater and knitting it up on bigger needles so that she could wear it to shelter her from the bitter cold north China weather. Shoes were more of a problem, as there was no way of making them bigger to fit growing feet! So Margaret prayed specifically for an answer to this problem, and was overjoyed when the answer came in a completely unexpected way. Someone else in the camp just walked up to her one day and said: 'I can't help noticing that your shoes are almost worn out. Try this pair and see if they fit you.' They did!

This was one of many direct answers to prayer, but God was at work in a specific way in that camp. For amongst their number was Eric Liddell, famous for being an Olympic gold medal winner back in the twenties. The film *Chariots of Fire* told the story of how Eric had refused to run on a Sunday because of his Christian principles. The race he refused to run was the 100 metres. But the 400 metres – a race he had never attempted – was to be run on a different day. Eric decided to enter for the race in spite of the fact that it was not his speciality. God honoured him for this. He won a gold medal, and set a world record. And his testimony lives on even today.

So this was the man who found himself in that Japanese camp where Margaret and her brother were struggling against the many hardships. He had found himself interned there through an unusual set of circumstances. He and his wife had planned to go to Canada, and Eric had sent his wife on ahead with their two children, expecting to follow very soon. But his plans were foiled. He was taken prisoner by the Japanese, and never made it to Canada. Separated from his wife – who was pregnant at the time – and from his two children he suffered the pain of being unable to look after them, or to spare them anxiety about his own welfare.

Instead, he decided to do all he could to help the young prisoners in the camp. Soon he became known as Uncle Eric, and the youngsters loved him. He organized hockey matches with makeshift hockey sticks, enthusing the contestants with his lively personality and refereeing their games. He would queue and carry for disabled or elderly people, in addition to seeing to his own needs. Everyone respected him – this great athlete in camp, who walked about in shorts helping people and doing good wherever an opportunity was found. He was a truly Christlike figure.

With other Christians in his dormitory he made a lamp out of a tiny tin, and with peanut oil and a little wick they would read the Bible and pray each morning, making sure to keep to one end of the room so as not to disturb the others. This way they kept their spirits high and their spiritual resources constantly renewed. God was real to them, and everyone who came into contact with them were aware of this. Their quiet witness shone out into the camp like a light which could not be hidden.

Then came a day when Uncle Eric began to suffer severe headaches. Gradually his condition worsened until he was finally admitted to the very sparsely equipped camp hospital. Some of the other Christians had formed a secret band in the camp, and Eric asked them if they would come and play 'Finlandia' outside his hospital window. It must have been an intensely moving moment for everyone who heard the music being played. "Be still, my soul, the Lord is on thy side; Bear patiently the cross of grief or pain; Leave to thy God to order and provide; In every change he faithful will remain." Soon after this, Eric died. The whole camp mourned this man of God, and strong men wept openly As for Margaret and the other young people, they could not believe that their Uncle Eric had been taken from them. Why had God allowed this to happen? What about his wife and children in Canada? Why had their prayers for their loved-ones' safety not been answered? So many questions and so much pain. It was a time for trusting and learning new but difficult lessons.

The Japanese would not provide any wood for a coffin, so Eric's body had to be carried in a flimsy covering to his grave outside the camp. And to this day there is still a beautiful stone memorial to him, donated by the citizens of his home – Perthshire in Scotland.

In the hot summer of 1945 the atom bombs were dropped on Hiroshima and Nagasaki, and after that the Japanese surrendered. The Americans were concerned about the prisoners in the camps. So they put food, clothes and medicines into drums and flew them to the camps. One morning during roll call, a plane appeared bearing American insignia. The prisoners went wild with excitement. For Margaret and her brother it was a moment they would never forget. At first they thought supplies were being dropped, and that was exciting enough. But then they saw legs appearing below the drums and realised that soldiers were being dropped into the camp. The Japanese guards made no attempt to prevent the Americans from taking over the camp, and everyone rushed out to meet the liberators.

The seven men who had been 'dropped' into the camp said: 'Watch your heads – the plane is coming round again and they are going to drop food for you!' What a treat it was for them all to find peaches, chocolates, coffee and medicines, as well as clothes and shoes – all dropped by parachute! These were unbelievable riches and their joy knew no bounds! Their dreadful ordeal was over.

When Margaret and her brother left camp they didn't know where their parents were. They had not seen them for five and a half years. But they were still in China, and through the kindness of the RAF the family were reunited, and eventually returned to England on a troop ship. In spite of the long years of separation, Margaret remembers how the closeness of the family was as precious as it had ever been. They all thanked God for His loving care of them and marvelled to think of all the hazards they had undergone and survived.

One might have expected that Margaret would have hesitated about ever again venturing into foreign lands! But later she was to meet and marry Philip, and the two of them went to the Philippines, where they worked as missionaries for twenty-five years. Now, in retirement, they devote their lives to reaching out to students from all over the world.

'GOT ANY BREAD?'

I first met Joanie Yoder when we shared a platform in a Surrey church, soon after the publication of one of my books. We were both about the same age, and I remember being fascinated by her American charm and beauty. As she told her story to the women gathered there, I sensed that here was a very special lady.

Joanie and her husband had been travelling on the London Underground, when a young man, clearly under the influence of drugs or drink, approached Joanie with a look of desperation on his face.

'Got any bread?' he begged. And Joanie, not knowing that this was an appeal for money, dived into her bag for a sandwich she had been saving for later. The young man ate the sandwich, but began to explain his plight to her. He was hooked on drugs, and was now almost penniless. Joanie's response was to ask him whether anyone had ever told him about Jesus. To her surprise he answered: 'Jesus? I pray to Him every day, but help doesn't come!'

Without a moment's forethought, she says, she found herself answering: 'Well thank God He's answering your prayers, for we can help you.' Feeling suddenly out of her depth, and wondering what she was going to say next, Joanie looked across at her husband Bill, who was sitting opposite. But all he gave her were a few subtle eye signals telling her to be careful!

'Just then the train jerked to a stop', she wrote later. 'It wasn't our stop, but the young man thought it was. Wanting to give me a fond farewell he leaned toward me and put his arms around me. 'We're not getting off just yet' I said, hoping he'd realize by the "we" that I was not alone. But since you're leaning on me, let me pray for you right now. "Yes please" he answered. With his ear in the region of my mouth and with other passengers (not to mention Bill) watching wide-eyed, I prayed the compassion of Christ into that ear. I prayed for the Lord to save him and to deliver him not only from drugs but from all sin, and to give him new life and hope.'

Joanie then invited the man to visit their family home in Reading. Sure enough, he eventually took her at her word, and turned up with several of his friends. As a result of this chance encounter, Joanie and Bill and their two daughters founded a drug and alcohol rehabilitation centre in their three-bedroomed home. So successful was their venture, that the family eventually moved it to Yeldall Manor on the outskirts of Reading. And today the centre is still flourishing, helping men aged 20 to 40 to stay off drugs and alcohol by seeking out the underlying reasons for their addictions.

Having met Joanie on that occasion, many years ago now, our paths were to cross again when we found ourselves living within a few miles of one another. She was a person from whom the love of God, and the joy of living for Him, shone brightly. Whenever we met, I went away feeling richer for having spent time with her.

In her book *Finding the God Dependent Life* Joanie tells of the various struggles and trials which had dogged her path both before and after founding Yeldall Manor. The hardest of all was to lose her husband Bill to cancer. She tells how she visited him daily in the Sue Ryder Home where he eventually died. She writes:

Each evening I would drive back to Yeldall Manor for a night's sleep, and each morning before driving back to the

Sue Ryder Home I would rise quite early to renew myself in the Lord. After making myself a mug of tea, I would sit in a comfortable chair with my Bible on my lap and watch the day dawn across the beautiful Yeldall lawns. This was not the time to get into absorbing Bible study or to make long-winded intercessions. This was the time to say very little and to allow Him to speak if He wished, a time to browse through familiar portions of Scripture and simply soak up God's reassurance and comfort. . . .

As she looked back over the years to the meeting which led to the founding of Yeldall Manor, Joanie remembered that it was, humanly speaking, only by chance that she and Bill had been travelling on the Underground in London that day. They had been given tickets for a concert, and although they did not particularly want to go, they had done so for fear of offending the donor of the tickets. Tracing the hand of God in her life, Joanie marvelled at the way in which God works His purposes out. Now she had to hold on in blind faith that there was a purpose in Bill's illness.

She quotes some words by Gladys Hunt which had always been a help to her:

I am inclined to believe that special resources are made available to us when we need them, but that our capacity to receive from God and others is determined by the integrity of our relationship to God beforehand. A person who has been regularly drinking at the fountain of living water knows where to go when he is parched and dry. Another, used to digging his own well, may struggle to find the path to the Fountain.

After Bill died, Joanie proved the truth of these words once again.

She was certainly a person who drank regularly at that fountain, and she knew where to go in this dark time of loss and sorrow.

The final test was to come some years later, when Joanie herself was diagnosed with cancer. Along with all her other friends, I was shocked to receive this news. Not Joanie, we cried! Not radiant, beautiful Joanie! But one year later, we were gathered for one of the most beautiful and moving funeral services we could remember. Dozens of former drug addicts and alcoholics turned out to say good-bye to this remarkable woman, who thirty years previously had reached out in love and compassion to an unkempt stranger on a London Underground train. Total strangers broke down and wept because they had heard about her from others, and realised that we had lost someone very special.

And Yeldall Manor's residential director said: 'Joanie was a remarkable woman. Up till recently, she still visited here regularly and was still very much involved in our work. She had a gift that when she spoke to you, you believed you were the most important person on this earth. And to her at that time, you were.'

SERENDIPITIES

At a time in my life when I was in contact with the sister-in-law of J. B. Phillips, the well-known Bible scholar and translator, I became especially interested in him for a number of reasons. In his book *The Wounded Healer*, Phillips writes very movingly of his own wilderness experience at the time of severe mental illness. His heart-rending description of the effect this illness can have, on only on the patient, but not all who have to stand helplessly by, touched a chord in many other sufferers. The honesty with which the book was written bore testimony to the author's faith in a God who causes us to triumph even in the most distressing of circumstances.

But no doubt, for most people, the name of J. B. Phillips is chiefly associated with his *Letters to Young Churches*. This book appeared when there was very little choice in the way of translations, and the King James Version was the only one in common use. In his work among young people, Phillips was finding that, beautiful and inspiring as he himself found the Authorized Version of the Bible, the antiquity of its language was proving to be a barrier for many of the newer generation of would-be Bible scholars.

It was a time when various intellectuals were giving voice to what was then called the 'new theology', and Phillips had been deeply stirred and angered by the news of a colleague who had taken his own life because his reading of these critical works had left him to conclude that his whole life-work had been founded on false assumptions. Pondering. the matter, J.B. came to the conclusion that those who wrote so cleverly and devastatingly about the Christian faith can have little personal knowledge of the living God.

Deeply concerned for the young people at that time under his care in wartime London, he undertook his work of translating the epistles into modern English so that they would be encouraged to discover the truth of the New Testament for themselves. When they were published, the *Letters to Young Churches* had an amazing effect on those who read them. To quote the author: 'The removal of the old varnish allowed the truth to reach them in a way it had not reached them before.'

But the second, and vitally significant effect was upon the translator himself. He tells how he found himself 'provoked, challenged, stimulated, comforted, and generally convicted of my previous shallow knowledge of Holy Scripture. I was confronted by eternal truths which my soul, however reluctantly, felt bound to accept.' Again and again, he stumbled upon unexpected evidence for his growing conviction that these letters were written out of dynamic, vibrant experience of a living, ever-present Saviour. These discoveries, he describes under the collective heading of 'serendipities' – a word which the dictionary defines as the 'faculty for making happy and unexpected discoveries by accident'.

The first important discovery was that the epistles could never have been written at all if there had been no Jesus Christ, no crucifixion and no resurrection. The more he thought about it, the more Phillips realized that it was unthinkable that any of this new courageous, joyful life could have originated in any kind of concocted story or wishful thinking.

The next thing he saw was that only a supernatural change in the lives of people in the church at Crinth could possibly explain the staggering transformation which had taken place in some of them. Having done some background reading into the history of the time, he was reminded that 'Corinth' was a byword in those wicked days for every kind of vice and depravity. He then read the words of Paul recounting some of the more repulsive sins to which human beings can sink, and saw that the apostle had gone on to say: 'And such were some of you!' 'What', asks the author, 'is supposed to have changed these men and women so fundamentally?' Suddenly it had become absolutely clear to him that human nature can only be fundamentally changed from within by the Holy Spirit. For people simply to 'turn over a new leaf' on this scale was unthinkable!

Some of the smaller serendipities J.B. discovered are especially moving and comforting. In translating the verse from Peter's epistle which the AV gives as 'Casting all your care upon him, for he careth for you' he saw that the word for 'casting' in the Greek is almost a violent word, suggesting that a man at the end of his tether might actually hurl aside his intolerable burden. The believer is being told to throw his humanly insupportable weight of care upon the only one who is strong enough to bear it, and to realize at the same time that God cares for him intimately as a person. Peter is actually saying that we, as individuals, are God's personal concern. The God revealed by Jesus Christ possesses wisdom and power beyond all human imagining, but never loses sight of any individual human being. What a serendipity!

The author of *Ring of Truth* – originally sub-titled 'A translator's testimony' – goes on to mention one thing after another which was revealed to him during the course of his translation work. He was constantly mining precious jewels from out of the storehouse of God's Word. His own life was transformed by these revelations, and he describes how, as a result of his studies, he came to move from the middle ground of a moderate faith, to the higher ground of spiritual certainty. And who can tell how many others lives were similarly transformed through reading *Letters to Young Churches* for themselves?

God, in His wisdom, chose to pour out all these treasures by means of letters: letters written by His appointed apostles and later included in the Canon of Scripture so that all might read them. And as for serendipities, when we read the Word of God with an open mind, asking the Holy Spirit to communicate to us through it, then every word He speaks to us is indeed a serendipity!

IN TANDEM WITH GOD

It was the end of one of the sunniest summers on record, and Anthony and Maggie Barker were riding along a main road in the Lake District on their white tandem. It was a cloudless sunny day, and they were in high spirits They had recently celebrated their golden wedding, and were on their way to revisit the beautiful location where they had spent their brief honeymoon 50 years earlier.

During those years which made up the half century, this couple had notched up a staggering list of achievements – together. During 27 years of devoted service as medical missionaries in Zululand, they had gradually transformed a dilapidated storehouse into a large, well-equipped general hospital. Their work attracted medical visitors from all over the world.

After a period of further work in South Africa, Anthony became consultant surgeon and Maggie senior physician, in charge of the casualty department of St. George's Hospital in London. Here they pioneered important work in the field of casualty care. When they retired from St. George's, they threw themselves full-time, into promoting their three lifelong passions – the spread of the gospel message, the plight of the Third World and the care of the environment.

Alongside all this activity, Maggie developed her talent for painting, mounting her own exhibitions and sales for charity. Anthony exercised his gift as a woodcarver, furniture-maker and calligrapher. The couple also took part in sponsored cycle trips, covering long distances on their white tandem, and negotiating high mountain ranges.

On this late summer day, as they pedalled happily along that road in the Lake District, one can imagine what memories must have been crowding their minds. Both looked younger than their years, and their faces were no doubt radiant with love for each other, for the countryside, and for their God.

They did not see the oncoming lorry until it was too late. They were both killed instantly.

Why? Why did God allow such a thing to happen to people who had spent every moment of their lives in service for Him? On the other hand we might react in quite a different way. What a wonderful was to go – together, at a moment of supreme joy, apparently without suffering. Even though they might have had another 20 years of fruitful life before them, it seems that God chose this moment for their joint service to be consummated in His presence.

In spite of the obvious tragedy, and the grief it must have brought to their many friends all over the world, and to their immediate family, no-one can deny that there was something beautifully fitting about the manner of their departure from this life.

Elijah was carried to heaven in a chariot of fire – but Anthony and Maggie rode to glory on a white tandem!

TIMELESS MOMENTS

Some years ago, when the 'charismatic movement' was at its height, I began to think seriously about what modern psychology calls 'altered states of consciousness'. People all around me were coming into experiences which could not be explained by any logical means. Nor could they then be related to anything in my own spiritual journey. In my reading I had come across varied accounts of semi-mystical happenings which puzzled and interested me. What did they mean, and how was it that some people came into such experiences and not others?

I was aware of a deepening spiritual hunger in my own life at that time, reaching out for a closer walk with God, and crying out to Him to show me how to fulfil His purposes for me in a fuller, richer way.

Then something happened to me which I have written about elsewhere, and which I shall not go into again now. But suffice to say that my search for some kind of answer to the meaning of such experiences became more intense, and I began to read even more widely on the subject. I soon discovered that there was indeed a unifying element for the kind of encounters with the eternal which can loosely be labelled 'mystical'. This was a sense of worthlessness, and an abandoning of the selfhood to God, followed by an awareness of a consuming love and an ecstatic joy that defies verbal expression.

The philosopher, historian and scholar F. C. Happold, who himself made such an investigation following an experience which changed his whole life, has summed it up like this:

> There are times when the awakened soul, craving for a revelation which will make sense of the riddle of the universe, of the apparent futility of life, and of its own inadequacy may feel that there is no answer, sick with longing, it can only cry out to God. But the desire is everything . . . suddenly the timeless moment is there, the morning stars sing together, a sense of utter joy, utter certainty and utter worthlessness mingle, and in awe and wonder it murmurs, I know.

He goes on to describe something which happened to him when he was an undergraduate at Cambridge. Suddenly, he says, the room with its shabby furniture and the fire burning in the grate seemed to be filled with a presence which, in a strange way, was about him and within him like light and warmth. He was overwhelmingly conscious of being possessed by Someone who was not himself, and yet he felt that he was more 'himself' than he had ever been before. He was filled with an intense, almost unbearable joy, and over all was a sense of peace and security and certainty. For he had met with the living Christ.

Compare this with a quotation from the writings of D. L. Moody, well-known American evangelist of a previous generation:

> I was crying all the time that God would fill me with his Spirit. Well, one day in the city of New York – oh, what a day! – I cannot describe it. It is almost too sacred an experience to name. (St. Paul had an experience of which he never spoke for fourteen years.) I can only say that God

revealed himself to me, and I had such an experience of his love that I had to ask him to stay his hand. I went preaching again.

The sermons were no different. I did not present any new truths. And yet hundreds were converted. I would not now be placed back where I was before that blessed experience if you should give me all the world – it would be as small dust in the balance.

The total difference between these two men, their religious background, their education, their conditioning, and hence their different way of expressing themselves is obvious. But both of them experienced a transforming encounter with God, and in both cases there was an initial yearning, a longing and a yielding. As I read what they had written, as well as the many examples of similar experiences as recounted by people from all backgrounds and all shades of Christian belief, I was brought back time and time again to a contemplation of the greatness of our God. How dare we try to confine Him to the narrow strait-jacket of our own limited vision, our own pre-conceived, stereotyped ideas!

How dare we mould Him to a pattern of our own making, expecting Him to conform to type as we so often do ourselves? He will have nothing to do with our small-minded attempts at uniformity; He will not be typecast, or regimented.

When we try to classify or categorise our experience of God, we are trying to harness the wind. When Jesus had accomplished all that the Father had sent Him to do, He sent His Holy Spirit –invisible, unpredictable, untameable – just as He said He would: 'The wind blows wherever it pleases. You hear its sound, but you cannot tell where it comes from or where it is going. So it is with everyone born of the Spirit.'

PART TWO

PREAMBLE

On a bright Autumn afternoon at around two o'clock, I handed my husband a cup of tea, and suggested that we catch a bus into town to take a leisurely look at an Art Exhibition in which he had two of his paintings on display.

On the following afternoon, at around the same time, I was sitting in the office of our local undertaker, being handed a catalogue of coffins from which to choose one for my beloved life partner. Numb with shock and disbelief, I stared at the pictures in the catalogue, while a friendly voice began to talk about prices and types of wood. A sense of complete unreality washed around me like a bad dream.

In the days that followed, while the sympathy cards poured in through the letterbox, and friends surrounded me with their love and concern, I was aware only of a dull ache. There was so much to be done, so many things to arrange, so many people still to be contacted.

Then out of one of the envelopes fell a little booklet about grieving in the 'How-to' series. Someone had handed me an identical booklet the previous day. Now, I wanted to throw the neat, carefully thought-out treatise across the room. Anger surged up in me, resulting in yet another outburst of tears. Even as I mopped them up, adding the sodden tissue to the ever-growing pile beside me, I knew that the little book would have informed me that shedding tears was good for me. That I should on no account try to hold them back. Just let them flow . . . As if I had any choice in the matter!

I felt then, and still do, that grieving is a strictly individual and personal process. That it is compounded of a lifetime of unique experience in whatever relationship it is that has been severed. That it is a journey which must be walked alone. There is no set pattern, no recipe for coping well. Oh yes, all the clichés are true in a measure, as all clichés are. I did feel as if I had lost a limb. I did feel that I had suddenly become half a person. Time does heal. But only up to a point, and never completely.

A phone call from the hospital asked if I would like to come and see my husband's body. While I hesitated, I was strongly advised by the kindly voice that I would later be glad I had done so. It was not true. The sight of the still, marble figure so nicely and neatly laid out only served to remind me of a similar occasion many years ago when I had stood looking down at the china-doll figure which was all that remained of a precious daughter. I wanted to remember my husband and lover as I had last seen him – leaning back in the familiar armchair as though he had just fallen asleep. His last words in answer to my question about the cup of tea had been: 'That would be nice . . .' The quiet words hung on the air as I reached for the telephone and dialled the emergency services . . .

The Christian clichés abounded, too. 'He's with the Lord' . . . 'What a lovely way to go . . .' 'God's timing is always perfect . . .' Again, all true, of course, and deeply comforting in their own way.

But if I had been asked exactly how I felt during those first dream-like days, I would have to admit to alternating waves of searing grief and a strange incredible joy. Years of shared experience had bonded us together in a way that no-one could ever take away. Incommunicable suffering had at times culminated in a silent clinging together in which words of any kind would have been futile.

And times of equally incommunicable joy had overwhelmed us during times of deep unity of thought and shared perception. To have experienced such love is a precious jewel I shall carry into eternity.

But there is a high price to pay for such closeness. For no-one can ever fill the gap. There are times when I yearn still for his close embrace, for his instinctive understanding of a particular need. We had somehow slipped into the habit each morning on waking of sitting up in bed and holding hands while we quietly talked over things that were on our minds. Or simply sat in quiet communion with each other, with no words required. Now there was no human hand to reach for. Nobody there on the other side of the bed . . .

There was an occasion early in my journey of grief, when I awoke in the night. And cried out to God to help me; to speak a word to me in my desperate loneliness. I put on the light and reached over to turn on my radio which is tuned in day and night to classical music. Maybe, I thought, there would be a Mozart piano concerto or one of my other favourites to calm me and speak peace to my soul. Instead, to my amazement, I heard a voice reading from a Psalm.

It was as though God reached down out of heaven and answered my prayer by speaking to me directly: 'My mouth praises you with joyful lips when I think of you upon my bed, and meditate on you in the watches of the night For you have been my help, and in the shadow of your wings I sing for joy. My soul clings to you, and your right hand upholds me . . .'

I began to reach out my hand each morning after that for the hand of God. I shared with him the pain and loneliness, and felt the indescribable joy of His presence flooding my soul with peace and comfort. And always I found that I had only to reach out for that hand to find it ready and waiting to reach out for mine.

I began to keep a journal in which I recorded my fluctuating feelings and thoughts as the days and the weeks went by. I wrote as though actually addressing my loved one, and these 'letters' brought me great comfort. I have recommended this idea to other grieving people, and share now some extracts from what I wrote, in the hope that others might find comfort from them. For to be able to identify with another's emotional journey is surely a strengthening thing.

The date on which my husband died was actually November 6th, and when, later on, I opened my *Daily Light* to read the verses for that day, I was amazed to find that this is what they were:

> I am the resurrection and the life: he that believeth on me, though he were dead, yet shall he live.
>
> God hath given to us eternal life, and this life is in his Son. He that hath the Son hath life, and he that hath not the Son hath not life.
>
> The Lord Himself shall descend from heaven with a shout, with the voice of the archangel, and with the trump of God: and the dead in Christ shall rise first: then we which are alive and remain shall be caught up together with them in the clouds to meet the Lord in the air: and so shall we ever be with the Lord. Wherefore, comfort one another with these words.
>
> When he shall appear, we shall be like him; for we shall see him as he is.
>
> [The body] is sown in dishonour; it is raised in glory; it is sown in weakness; it is raised in power.
>
> If I go and prepare a place for you, I will come again, and receive you unto myself; that where I am, there ye may be also.

Now, every year on the anniversary of his death, I read those words and wonder afresh at the way God made each promise so very personal for me. The verse about the body sown in dishonour and raised in glory was especially precious. No longer did I need to think about his poor body as I had last seen it – lying on the floor as the paramedics struggled to resuscitate it – but in its resurrection glory, radiant with life and perfect in knowledge. I began to write my journal not long after the funeral was over.

LETTERS TO MY LOVE

NOVEMBER 20TH

After the longest summer on record, a late, late autumn. Only a few days now to December, yet the birch trees outside the kitchen window have only just turned to gold. Still in full leaf, their shimmering foliage fill the whole window frame with a luminous glow, lighting up the room and taking me by surprise each time I enter, so that I have felt compelled to paint them.

On the day that you died (can it be only two weeks ago?) those birches were green – almost an unnatural sight on a November day. It was as though autumn delayed her coming especially for you. Because you never liked the autumn. Leaf fall and the turning of the year seemed to increase your natural tendency for melancholy. You struggled each year reluctantly into winter, painting the occasional river scene with the bright, reflected trees, or sketching from the windows.

You were spared all that, my darling, this year. But the glories of heaven hold no seeds of melancholy, no sadness. There are no shadows on those celestial fields, no hidden menace in the hedgerows. No dark mysteries, no pain, no tears. Only unalloyed pleasures for evermore.

For eye has not seen, nor ear heard, the things that God has prepared for those who love Him. 'In your presence is fullness of joy: at your right hand are pleasures for evermore . . .'.

NOVEMBER 22ND

What a wealth of pleasure we enjoyed together during that last, long summer! It began with those two glorious weeks in St. Ives back in May in our flat above the Porthmeor beach. What magnificent high seas there were! What brilliant changes of light and colour! How we revelled together in all that colour – purples, greens and blues, fuchsia pink and vivid turquoise – as we snatched precious moments together. With mugs of tea we'd sit, early in the morning, eulogising about all that beauty. Soon we were reaching for our sketchbooks in an attempt to capture some of it before the light began to change too rapidly.

I went for my paints, and you laughed indulgently at my obsessive need to go straight for colour every time. You were often content to draw, or work with coloured pencils, reserving painting times for the evenings - or earlier, if the weather kept us in.

You haunted the galleries, talking art with the folk you met there each year. Or you sat on the island studying the rock formations (you could never get enough of them) and drawing, drawing . . .

Meanwhile, L. and I sat in the harbour, or on the beach; or we browsed around craft shops and fairs. Our threesome pattern worked well this way A blessed relief after all the trauma and heartache of the past year. But there were times when you and I yearned to spend more time together.

I remember a morning of strong wind and high seas. L. had decided not to go out, as there was a threat of rain. So you and I went out together like two birds released from a cage! We walked up the cobbled streets with our arms around each other, and we kissed on a quiet corner like young lovers. For a glorious hour we dived into little galleries and shops, savouring the precious intimacy.

Such memories never die. And no-one can ever take them away from me . . .

NOVEMBER 25TH

A card came this morning, enclosing a smaller, printed one entitled 'Togetherness'. Expecting to find some sentimental verses, I merely glanced at it initially. But on closer inspection I found that it expressed almost perfectly how I feel about you now. Or rather how you would be speaking to me now if you had a mortal voice:

'Death is nothing at all. I have only slipped away into the next room. I am I, and you are you. Whatever we were to each other, that we are still . . .'

Oh, my darling – yes, yes, yes! My heart thrills to the knowledge that this is so. Our closeness, our companionship continues, even though your physical presence is absent. Sometimes I catch myself talking aloud to you, or reaching out to you as I move about from room to room.

Only this morning I thought that maybe while the autumn colours are so vibrant I would go alone to Pangbourne, walk by the river, stop off for coffee in the little café, and simply remember all the lovely moments we had spent there together. I remembered how, not long before you died, you had been looking at those colourful paintings by David Schlee – humps of landscape, clumps of trees on the Chilterns – all in vivid greens, yellows and oranges. Some were heavy with darker colours and menacing forms. You loved them, though for me they had no real appeal.

So while I painted a conventional river scene, you drew the hills beyond and later transposed them to canvas. It was only the second oil-painting you had done in twenty years! And you were so pleased with the result. Early one morning you thought of a frame which might fit it, and still in your pyjamas, ran down to the kitchen to try it out. Soon it was hanging on the wall, and we were sitting like a couple of kids on the sofa, admiring it and holding hands . . .

Every morning, as soon as we were awake, we tuned in to Radio Three and sat up together.

'Shall we have a cuppa now?'

'I'll get it.'

'No, I will.'

And then we talked, sharing our views and thoughts, our plans for the day. And holding hands.

On that first morning without you, my first conscious thought was that you were not there. Not there to reach for my hand. Not there to hear my voice or for me to hear yours.

I shan't go down to Pangbourne alone. Not yet, not today.

DECEMBER 1ST

'Shall we have a day in London? We haven't been since the Spring!'

'Are you sure? I'll get my diary and see.'

Always eager to check out facts, figures, dates or details of any kind in one of your many record books, you hopped out of bed and into your den.

'You're right. It was March.'

'Next Thursday, then?'

You wrote the date in your diary. A day in London was one of our favourite things to do, and had been since the day we retired. I shall always remember that particular outing as a shining day. From beginning to end it was, for me, a day shot through with joy of a particularly luminous quality. A day of heightened awareness . . .

On the train my attention was drawn toward a group of people – two women and a little girl – whose presence flooded me with a peculiar upsurge of warmth. I was aware that my love was reaching out to them, as though I was being drawn into their warm circle, sharing in their love of life and of each other.

I guessed that they were on their way to London to buy a bridesmaid outfit for the child, who sat by her mother, opposite the future bride. The face of the mother was beautiful, Madonna like, and the sound of her voice and her laughter reached out to me like music. The child nestled against her like a bird in a nest. Later, in the Festival Hall, something very similar happened We sat together, you and I on a cream leather sofa up in the gallery area, eating our lunch and listening to the music group which played in the foyer below. Then a young woman came alone and unpacked a bag of painting material near where we were sitting. Leaning on the parapet just in front of us, she proceeded to paint colourful, free-movement sketches of the group below. You had your little pocket sketchbook out, and you did a quick outline of her at work.

Then along came a young man with a child in a pushchair, and it soon became clear that he was the husband of the artist. Soon members from the music group arrived to discuss terms for what was obviously a commissioned publicity poster. As they talked together, one of the musicians – a young man with a beard – reached out and took the baby in his arms, holding it with loving care. The child's father glowed with paternal pride; the mother looked on as she began to clear away her paints. . . .

I said: 'There are so many lovely people in the world . . .' And you nodded in warm agreement.

We always went our separate ways after lunch in the Festival Hall. (You called it our club!) You went on up to the poetry library, and from there up to the Charing Cross Road to do your 'bookshop crawl'. . . I headed for Westminster Bridge, arriving at the Abbey just in time for the three o'clock call to prayer . . .

Sitting only a few yards from the altar, I noted the beauty of the tapestry altar cloth which today consisted of three concentric circles representing the Greek letters Alpha and Omega. The central circle depicted a maze, in the centre of which were the simple word: 'I AM'

When I had allowed the wonder of this to sink in, I went on my way for my customary walk through St. James's Park, down the Mall to Green Park, over Picadilly and down New Bond St. We met, as usual, for our meal together in a restaurant nearby.

A kiss and a hand clasp, then I asked you if you had a good day.
'Yes, but I'm very tired. And you?'
'I've had a beautiful day. A kind of golden day . . . I can't explain . . .'
You smiled and your face lit up.
'I'm so glad. Oh, I love you so much.'
'And I love you.'
It was to be our very last outing to London.

DECEMBER 3RD

I tried not to be anxious about your increasing tiredness, and looking back I wonder at the overriding sense of joy I felt during these days, in spite of the underlying unease. It was though the very brilliance of my strange joy cast a shadow close behind me which I was determined to ignore. It's the only way I can explain the strangeness of those days. Perhaps it was simply that God was surrounding me with His love, encompassing me about with His presence in a special way to prepare me for the sorrow ahead.

In the Abbey bookshop that day I had picked up Michael Mayne's *Sunrise of Wonder*, thought about buying it but went away having made a note of its title and publisher. Recently I was able to borrow it from the library; and have been reading a little of it each day.

Time and again I have wanted to read bits out to you, and often I have thought that it is your kind of book rather than mine. For though much of it is rather beyond my intellectual grasp, I know it would not have been beyond yours. And there is even a section on Kettles Yard in Cambridge, which you loved so much . . .

Writing on the role of the artist, Michael Mayne points out that the great imaginative artists have taken the commonplace of human experience and distilled them, intensified them, so that we see the familiar transfigured. Samuel Palmer wrote: 'I must paint the hills so as to give us promise that the country beyond them is paradise.'

This ability to look at things through an inner eye with a joyful intensity was something which set you apart from those who paint only what they see with the 'outer eye'. I remember how A.S. Byatt had described herself as someone who saw everything too bright, too fierce, too much. She mentioned Samuel Palmer too, referring to his 'over-loaded magic apples', and to William Blake who saw infinity in a grain of sand. 'This vision of too much makes the visionary want to write – or paint, or compose, or dance, or sing . . .'

'I don't want to paint pretty pictures' you often said. And you tended to become exasperated with folk who didn't understand that. At St. Ives you could immerse yourself in the lives of the artists who formed the 'Art Colony' of the thirties and forties – Ben Nicholson, Barbara Hepworth, Barnes Graham and the rest.

You would come home from Cornwall with your sketchbooks full of detailed drawings of rocks or designs developed from intricate markings of tide movements in the sand. Those who expected to see 'pretty scenes' would be disappointed. For what they did not understand was that you looked at everything with that intensely joyful inner eye . . .

Michael Mayne wrote that to look truly at anyone or anything is to love. And you – with your one good eye – knew how to look like that.

But there is a price to pay for all true creativity, as every visionary knows.

DECEMBER 21ST

Not everyone realized you had gone through life with the sight of only one eye. This slight deformity tended to give you quite a fierce look. I remember how difficult it was for me to come to terms with that in the early days. The effect was to make it appear that you were averting your gaze during a conversation; and I, who always need to make eye contact with those I talk to, found that disconcerting too.

But how much you saw – really saw with that one good eye! The incredible graphic detail of your drawings bears witness to that. And how much love, or humour – or anger – could be expressed in it without a word being spoken! How I thank God that your eyesight remained unimpaired right up to the end; that you missed nothing of the visual treasures this life has to offer . . . Yet how often those eyes were filled with tears, your shoulders bowed with melancholy, your brow clouded not only with all that residual nagging pain you had from the shingles which had attacked you ten years previously, but with the pain of inner conflicts and secret sorrow . . .

At such times I was powerless to help you, and that fact tore me apart too. I would long to take you in my arms and soothe away the pain, but it was too deep for any human comfort. And often I risked a rebuff if I attempted to reach out to you. That hurt me more than anything, because your arms were an unfailing source of comfort to me whenever I needed you. Why could not my arms meet your need too? Such questions are futile, yet they haunt and torture . . .

Oh, my darling, I felt so helpless at those times, so excluded. For I knew only too well what lay behind much of the pain.

But this morning, in my daily reading, on this, the shortest day of the year, came the reminder that we who are still clothed in mortal flesh 'groan and travail in pain' – longing to be unclothed of that flesh and re-clothed in glory – 'that mortality might be swallowed up of life'

What a glorious picture – to think of all the human pain and frailty of our mortal lives being actually swallowed up, not by death, but by vibrant, shining, eternal life!!

How can I grieve for you? How can I feel anything but pure joy that the one I loved so much is, at this very moment, so gloriously alive? And not only alive, but radiantly, cloudlessly fulfilled and whole!

But I do grieve, of course. There are times when I walk around the house murmuring: 'Sweetheart. Oh, my sweetheart.' And other times when I am overwhelmed with such a terrible sense of desolation that I cry like a child – not quietly, but noisily, unable to control the surge of violent pain, the raging emotional turmoil. Afterwards, I feel physically battered and inwardly drained of strength, struggling to remind myself that "tears are for healing". But it is usually not until several days later that I convince myself of this.

And now it is nearly Christmas

DECEMBER 30TH

It's all over – my first Christmas alone. You never really enjoyed those big, extended family gatherings, anyway. We always kept close to each other at the various parties, and you often said you wish we could spend Christmas quietly at home, as we used to do while you were in the Ministry. We couldn't be away from our churches, then, because of the seasonal services. But things were different once you retired. So this year I faced a family party without you. No-one seemed to know what to say to me. I kept with L., but felt that the others were almost avoiding us. Then Tim – who would be about thirty-two, now – came over and simply put his arms first around me, then round L. He didn't speak; just held us close. It was a precious moment. If only others would understand that there are no need for words . . .

I've been thinking again about the way I reacted to the little booklets on 'how to grieve' I was surprised at the vehemence of my own reaction.

'I don't want to be told how to grieve!' I cried to the empty room. 'I know about grief. I am acquainted with grief. I have lived with grief of one kind and another for half my life. And with God's help I shall live through this ultimate grief in my own way.'

I remember when a certain 'professional' lady expressed concern to me that a close neighbour of ours was not grieving "properly" for his wife, feeling a sense of exasperated outrage. What did this person know of the inner sanctum of this man's life? Had she observed the long, slow journey toward death that this devoted couple had walked, or seen the gradual deterioration of the loved body and mind; or shared the deep pain as this man faced the prospect of separation and loneliness?

God prepares us for the tragedies of life in His own way, giving us intimations of darkness, but counter-balancing them with shafts of light, and the promise of His unfailing presence. You and I went through that slow process in the year that led up to Frankie's death. Sometimes the shafts of light were radiant with the miracle of joy, and so it is for me now. This is something which has to be experienced to be understood.

I suspect that even when death is sudden, as it was with you, a measure of preparedness is given us to cushion the blow. This was certainly true for me. I still remember the day – about two years ago when the first warning shadow fell across my path. There was no specific reason for it. But suddenly the blue of the summer sky was full of menace and threat. I remember saying to a close friend that I felt as though a dark chasm had opened up at my feet. But why was I so full of fear and dread? I could not explain it.

That shadow hung over me for months, robbing me of my inner joy. I clung to you in a way I had never done before, drawing strength from the warmth of your love and the closeness of your body. A dark time, yet through it all the grace of God was unfailing, and the daily consciousness of His presence was like a rock beneath my feet. Deep in my subconscious mind, I believe my grieving for you began then, my darling. And now that the dark tide has reached the shore of my mind, as it were, I know the presence of God in a deeper and fuller way. The shining of His nearness comes to me each time, like a door opening on to a dark room. And so I am never alone.

JANUARY 1ST

The beginning of a new year – a new chapter in my life.

How glad I am that we were able to have that one last holiday on our own just before you died! I remember booking it with such determination, feeling that nothing should be allowed to prevent us from enjoying what had been denied us for so long. What a precious time it was in so many ways!

The October sunshine was warmer than it had been in May. Once more we sketched and painted, walked and talked, read the books we had borrowed from the local library. You had your usual biographies of the artists you loved, and you read bits out to me from time to time.

I had borrowed a kind of anthology compiled by the author Catherine Cookson – not because I was familiar with her novels, but because this collection of her poems, drawings and comments on life looked interesting. What a remarkable woman I found her to be! But there was one poem in particular which I found moving in the extreme. In it she asks how she would cope if ever she were to lose her husband – if there were no voice to speak with her when she awoke in the morning, no hand to hold. I read the lines out to you, telling you how close they were to my own fears and feelings:

Don't leave me, beloved, on this plane
Without your hand to grasp in the night
And your voice to wake me from sleep
And your love to wrap my day in kindness . . .

When I had read out these opening lines of the poem, I couldn't go on. We clung to each other, not with sadness, but with gratitude.

The high point, the climax of that week came the day before we were due to leave for home. It was a glorious day, and I wanted to walk round the island immediately after breakfast. I sensed that you

LETTERS TO MY LOVE

didn't feel quite up to it, and you urged me to go alone and meet you an hour later in the harbour. I sang to myself as I walked, hardly able to contain my joy and delight. So much beauty! Cobalt sky, the Atlantic romping in, all turquoise, jade and foaming white, and the island as green and fresh as midsummer. And the air so pure and crystal clear, inviting me to inhale great draughts of it. At the far end, down among the massive black rocks, a seal came in to swim and play. I chatted with one of the other walkers who had also sighted the seal. Then up to the very top to stand by the little mariner's chapel of St. Nicholas and absorb the whole panoramic feast.

In the harbour you were waiting sitting in the sun watching the boat. Over the years you had spent hours up on the island, studying the massive rock formations and drawing them over and over again. Today you were content to stay on more level ground and enjoy the endless variations of colour, movement and sound in the harbour.

Walking later along the quayside, we made for the little continental-style café at the far end. Tables and chairs were set out in the sun, and although we had intended only to have coffee, we found ourselves looking at the menu – and then, almost in unison we said:

'What about lunch – Crab Breton salad and a glass of wine?'

How we enjoyed that simple, impromptu meal, eaten in warm, mellow sunshine and with our favourite view of the distant harbour to feast our eyes on too!

But you were tired when we arrived back at the flat, and when I said how much I'd love to walk up to Clodgy Point that afternoon, I was not surprised when you once more urged me to go alone. You would go down to the Penwith gallery, and rhe Saltash, you said. You knew the proprietors there, and had not yet called in to see them.

Looking back, I still can't explain the sense of exhilaration I felt as I set off – except that I felt totally free, and full of praise to God for all the blessings that were mine. All the secret suffering of the past years – pain which had isolated us in a kind of cell of loneliness which we did not expect anyone to understand – all were somehow swept up into the hillside by the cleansing wind, by the sheer majesty of the towering rocks and sound of the sea crashing far below.

I ran and walked and climbed – my sketch bag swinging on my shoulder – impatient to reach the summit, for I planned to paint up there when I arrived. I talked aloud as I climbed, thanking God over and over again for the magnificence of His creation, for our deep, unending love, for the beautiful week we had enjoyed.

The view from the top was breathtaking. With my back to St. Ives, I faced the five or six visible rocky headlands which tapered away toward Zennor and beyond. The wind was quite strong up there, but I settled down with my sketchbook and paints, and was soon at work.

What a total experience of delight! I was still a beginner as a watercolourist, and was never quite sure what you thought about my efforts, but to paint outside was a total experience of delight. The sound of the wind and sea; the feel of salty air on my skin, the taste, the touch of it. The visual grandeur, inviting my eyes to explore each miniscule detail – rust red bracken on the headland, great rocks embedded in the cliff tops as well as down on the beaches; ancient stone which had not moved or changed for centuries . . . and the sea, the sea, the rainbow-coloured sea.

An hour or so later, I was on my way back to St. Ives, back to the flat and to you.

'Had a good time?'

'Fantastic – just fantastic. I wish you could have been up there with me. Look, I did a painting . . .'

I looked at your tired face, and felt a moment of misgiving.

Four weeks later you would be dead.

JANUARY 4TH

Joy and sorrow, it has been said, are but different sides of the same coin. That must be why my heart feels like this these days – a coin that is constantly being tossed from one side to the other.

Sometimes I am lifted up by such a surge of joy – as though on the crest of one of those Atlantic breakers – a joy so intense that I am almost ashamed to own it. Yet I know it is God-given, like the touch of an angel's wing. I feel myself bathed in the warm glow of a holy presence.

But there are days when the waves seem to dash me against the rocks, and I long for your touch, for the comfort of your arms, the reality of your presence. My throat aches with unshed tears, and I simply cannot believe that you are gone beyond my physical reach . . .

JANUARY 6TH

Why do I used the word 'shame' in connection with this strange joy – a joy I cannot explain or account for? But I can account for it, I can explain it, because I know what the source of it is! How often have I spoken to others of that paradoxical joy – the joy that Paul experienced in the midst of persecution and sorrow; the joy of the saints down the ages who have suffered for His name. And did not Jesus Himself, "for the joy that was set before Him" go to the cross, despising the shame?

Psalm 34 has often been a source of uplift not only for me, but for countless others:

My soul makes its boast in the LORD;
Let the afflicted hear and be glad.
Look to Him and be radiant
So your faces shall never be ashamed.
The angel of the LORD encamps
Around those who fear Him, and delivers them.

O taste and see that the LORD is good;
Happy is the man who takes refuge in Him!

Now, when I awake each morning, my darling, I cannot reach for your hand. Instead I reach for the hand of God, feeling Him instantly ready to reach out His hand toward me; to listen and to speak with me. Even when my first waking thought may be heavy with sorrow, my heart lifts with joy at the prospect of making contact with such a strong and loving God.

The LORD is near to the broken-hearted
And saves the crushed in spirit.
Oh magnify the LORD with me
And let us exalt His name together.

You. My beloved, are in the realms of eternal glory, continually praising, endlessly exalting His name. So my poor heart, still in its mortal frame, feels the privilege of joining its voice with yours! And do I still say I can't explain my joy – or dare to feel ashamed of it?

JANUARY 12TH

Today I met G. for coffee, and she told me of a most inspiring sermon she'd heard last Sunday. The preacher suggested that our lives are often formless and shapeless, with unresolved areas and tracks of unacknowledged failure. We look back sometimes and feel perplexed and confused, looking for pattern and purpose and finding none. Yet God the Creator-Father moves constantly above the chaos and darkness of our lives, giving form and substance and meaning, bringing life out of what seems useless, and light out of darkness. He gathers up all the loose ends as it were and draws them together by the skill of His creative power; giving beauty for ashes, and making crooked paths straight.

Thus, if we offer each day to Him, and ourselves in it, to do with us and through us what He will, then we, too, will touch people and situations with a creativity which echoes His.

Isn't this what Paul is saying in Romans 8:28? That no matter how much of darkness and failure there may be in our lives, God works it all together for good, using the very darkness to bring forth light, and turning sorrow into joy?

This is how it works in painting, too, of course, as you were often at pains to point out. The 'negative spaces' enhance the positive forms; the dark tones bring forward the light areas. The picture comes alive through these contrasts.

I am so conscious, just now, of that divine creativity at work in me, and my prayer is that it may spill out, in some small measure, into the world around me.

JANUARY 14TH

I know you constantly did battle with this sense of meaninglessness which threatened to engulf you at times. You found refuge in poetry, writing a little yourself, and reading a great deal of work by modern poets. I have to confess that this troubled me – for I felt that the kind of poetry you enjoyed only served to feed your melancholy. But this need of yours was akin to your hunger for the abstract in art and sculpture. Few of our evangelical friends could understand this need. There was something in you that made it necessary to portray the hidden menace in the landscape, the subtle distortion in shapes and forms.

One of your paintings has as its central focus a huge, towering rock in a Cornish landscape. You have distorted the shape, exaggerating the existing rugged shape into the semblance of a gaping monster. Below it, the fragile sea pinks grow among the grass, painted with precise skill and delicacy. Explaining to another minister your need to paint in this way, I was given an almost reproachful reply:

'Could he not have depicted it as the Rock of Ages?'

For you, the cross of Christ was central to all that you did or thought. And the Rock of Ages was indeed the source of your strength – the very means of your survival. But you were also keenly aware of the darkness that lies just below the surface of the world's glittering cover.

I found this poem which you wrote not long before you died:

To express the inexpressible
Having tasted of the spring
Where time meets eternity
And the mind leaps
In joyous recognition.

You never, in all your search for meaning in the dark valleys of life, lost sight of the ultimate meaning that lies in God Himself. This was the source of all your pastoral work – your preaching, your care of people. And this is why you were such an inspiration to all who knew you. You were a man in whom the love of God dwelt deeply, reaching out to all who came into contact with you. Your strength lay in your acute sensitivity, but in that sensitivity lay complex, and sometimes conflicting emotions. In it lay the capacity for compassion, the propensity for pain or joy.

JANUARY 16TH

But you yourself were a gentle man! Nearly every letter I received in the weeks following your death said so. And of course, it was true. I still feel that gentle presence all around me, and hear your soft footfall on the stairs . . .

You were a man with a great capacity for love, and I was privileged to be the chief beneficiary of that love – I, and our two precious daughters. Oh, with what a great love you loved us . . . I sometimes felt I would be nothing, would disappear like a shadow, or a reflection, without your love to give me meaning and identity. That is why I dreaded your passing with such a sense of foreboding. I was convinced that I would be totally consumed by grief. I reckoned, of course, without the wonders of God's grace.

Only a few nights after you had gone, just as I was falling asleep, the lines of a hymn came to me almost as if they were spoken by God Himself:

> The clouds you so much dread
> Are big with mercy and will break
> In blessings on your head.

God certainly does work in mysterious ways His wonders to perform. He took that great capacity for love of yours and used it to touch the lives of so many people. He used the pain, the regret, the longing to give and receive love which seemed to be denied you. (You will know what inner landscape I am referring to now.) God took all that and transmuted it into the kind of creative love which brought souls to new birth. For you they were drawn to Christ Himself, receiving the knowledge of His love through you.

Did He not say, 'I, if I be lifted up will draw all men unto me?'

You lifted Him up – in your preaching and in your pastoral care of your flock – as well as in your life. The redemptive love of the crucified Christ was what they saw in you. A love transformed through suffering.

> 'I loved him', they said
> 'A lovely man', they wrote.
> 'A gentle man . . .'

JANUARY 20TH

It gives me such comfort to know that you have all the answers, now, to the many questions that dogged your earthly path, and mine. I have been reminded this morning that when Job confronted God and regaled Him with questions regarding suffering, he received no answer. Instead, God showed Job Himself.

Maybe in heaven that is all we shall need: to see Him face to face. No questions will be necessary, for we shall know as we are known. Oh, the wonder of it all! And you, my darling have already entered into that wonder. As for me, I think I can honestly say that I can live without answers for the present, but I cannot live without Him . . .

JANUARY 22ND

The Coroner rang to say that your ring had been found at the hospital, and would I please come and collect it. After nine or ten weeks of believing that it was where I had asked to have it left – on your dear hand where I had placed it forty-five years ago . . .

When I had put the phone down, I burst into convulsive sobs, walked around the kitchen crying out: 'I didn't want it taken off, I didn't want it taken off . . .'

That ring symbolised so much of our oneness and closeness, the lovely bond of our married life together I had often thought over the past few weeks, how glad I was that I had asked for it to be left on your hand. But now, with the ring back in my possession, I can feel at peace again, having wept my way through a whole day because of it. I have stopped picturing it on the lovely, gentle, sensitive hand I loved so much, and have begun to think about wearing it on mine.

But I will go on remembering how I was caught unawares by that overwhelming – and totally unexpected – tide of grief.

JANUARY 30TH

I have a photo of you now, on the window ledge just above my desk. I came across it in an old album, and I knew it was just what I was looking for. Probably taken by me in a boat in Poole Harbour, it has captured perfectly the essence of what you were. You are wearing a green sweater, and you are turning round to face me in that boat with a look of warmth and happiness on your face. With your head slightly on one side, you are smiling straight into my eyes. When I draw back my curtains each morning, that smile greets me lovingly . . .

In the photo, both your hands are clearly visible, the left one holding the boat trip ticket has the sun shining directly on it, lighting up the wedding ring. Sometimes, when I am writing or painting I look up and catch your eye. You seem to be looking on encouragingly – as you always were in life. If I'm disappointed with a painting, your look says: 'Never mind, darling. You've had a go!' If I'm feeling particularly low, you say: 'Be happy!'

JANUARY 31ST

I finally came to a solution about your wardrobe. At first I couldn't bear to open the door. The sight of your jackets and trousers, your best suit and your raincoat tore me apart. I wanted to bury my face in the tweed of your jacket but dare not subject myself to such desolation. Should I ask someone to clear the wardrobe for me? Or should I simply go on leaving the door firmly closed?

One day I decided to turn off my feelings – like a light switch – and do the job myself. I began to pile the things on the bed ready to pack them into a bag for a charity shop. Suddenly I knew what I should do. I selected a few things – the ones you had worn most recently during the long summer, light jackets and trousers I had loved to see you in – and hung them back in the wardrobe. I hung the tweed jacket beside them, and then went to my own wardrobe and came back with coats and jackets to hang alongside yours. Now

I can go to the wardrobe for my own things and it feels right to see your things there, too.

I do believe that decisions about these things is an entirely personal, individual thing. It has taken me nearly three months to arrange the bedroom in exactly the way that feels right for me. It is my room now – but you are still around!

FEBRUARY 2ND

I've left your 'den' almost exactly as it was the day you died. Your watch and your reading glasses are still on the desk and all the comfortable clutter that you liked to surround yourself with is still there. Pebbles, bits of rock or rope picked up off beaches. Pieces of driftwood, most of which you had drawn several times over in different lights; piles of postcards (mostly prints of your favourite artists); poetry magazines and posters, a map of the Thames, and photos of Cornish engine houses are attached to the walls with bits of Blu Tack.

There are folios of drawings stacked up in every conceivable space, piles of sketchbooks, all neatly labelled, and one canvas already drawn out in pencil ready for painting. And of course there are sermon notes all meticulously labelled and filed away in a special cabinet. They represent years of study and pastoring, and for the time being, I shall not touch them . . . There are books everywhere, of course, at least 3,000 of them.

Sometimes I have taken a close friend up there and said: 'Take a look around, and you'll get some idea of what kind of man he was.' It's often not what they expect, of course, because few of them understood what a complex person you were. When they looked for traditional paintings, they were disappointed. They were puzzled by your brightly coloured abstracts, and by drawings which seemed to contain twisted shapes and distortions. There was one drawing in particular you had done from the upstairs window, featuring a Scots pine in the garden below. It was rather an odd tree, with most of its branches down one side, and the sun always rose just behind it, making odd shapes of darkness and light.

On one of your birthdays you did a brightly coloured sketch of that tree, and underneath the drawing you wrote:

'A birthday effort – odd, but satisfying. It says something about me, I suppose! A bit lop-sided?'

FEBRUARY 3RD

I've thought a lot about that sketch you did and the note you wrote beneath it. Were you trying to verbalise that inner conflict again? The drawings and paintings you developed from that original sketch all went one step further than displaying 'lop-sidedness'. They indicated a constant magnetic pull toward an almost obsessive creativity. Early in life you faced up to the fact that you must make a choice. Either you surrendered your life to the pursuit of Art – or to the service of God. You knew you had to make a choice – for 'no man can serve two masters'. . .

You chose the latter – but I believe you struggled all your life to subordinate your creative gift. For it was no ordinary gift, no mere talent, or craftsman's facility. It was a driving force. All true artists would know what you had to contend with. Many a relationship has been broken and many marriages have floundered because of this driving force which demands total commitment. I had to watch this conflict at work, and to absorb its repercussions, suffering with you in your struggle to survive it. But I've come full circle, haven't I, in this conversation with you, because it was this very sense of inner conflict which made it necessary for you to paint – and for me to write.

Even now, as I drive my pen relentlessly on, I feel the relief, the release of creative energy. I need to write. You needed to paint. It was a common factor which brought us together in the first place. It was a union ordained by God . . .

One of the surprisingly clear messages that came to me after your death was that God was telling me it was time to lay down a burden. I found myself turning to that page in *Reaching for God*, written twenty years ago, where I describe how I felt when we first met.

> As he came into the room, my first reaction was one of surprise. Although he was, in fact, only in his late twenties, he looked much older. Dark-haired and wearing horn-rimmed spectacles, he had the closed-in look of a recluse. As I made small talk with him, I thought to myself: 'Who could ever reach him? Who could ever break through that shell of defence he puts up against the world, and set the man inside free?' Yet in spite of his forbidding countenance, it was a gentle face, the face of a man who had suffered. To my unspoken question: 'Who could ever reach him?' the answer was already forming in my mind: 'I could, Lord, if that's what you want me to do!

I believe God gave me a task to fulfil. It was to contain heights of pure joy and depths of despair. I was to receive the deep love and devotion of very special man – a man who would need me and be emotionally dependent on me for the rest of his life. It was a task with which I feel privileged to have been entrusted.

FEBRUARY 5TH

Did I ever really 'reach' you – ever really understand? Do we poor earthly creatures ever make vital contact with each other? Or are we always essentially alone? 'Each man an island' etc.? One thing is certain: even the closest, happiest married couples impose restrictions on one another, albeit unconsciously. And even in these days of so-called 'sexual equality', it's still the woman whose individuality is most likely to be diminished. The greater the love, the greater the desire to meet the hidden needs of her partner, so great in proportion will be her inner struggle to survive as a fully integrated person.

I have been reading some of your poems, and feeling depressed by the dark tone of some of them. Having coffee with G. the other day, I talked to her about this and found myself unburdening to her, as I often do.

'Why was my love not enough?' I asked 'Why?'

'Because love never is', she answered quietly.

Another message came to me – this time from someone I did not know, but who had known you in your pastoral capacity. God had prompted him to write and say that He had undoubtedly called you home at not only the exact right time for you, but at the exact right time for me too.

I remembered how another early reaction to your death had been to cry out silently: 'Who am I now? I have to rediscover my true identity. I have to liberate my essential self . . .'

And I, who had feared I would dissolve like a shadow if ever you were taken from me, suddenly became aware that something totally different from this was about to take place.

And now a letter from a near-stranger seemed to shed a new light on my path.

FEBRUARY 18TH

Your birthday, sweetheart. I thought I was ready for it, but I wasn't. Mary rang me to ask did I know there was a service being broadcast from Upton Park? They were singing 'Crown Him with many crowns', which we sang at your funeral. I was already struggling to hold back the tears. Now the floodgates burst open. And the clear blue and gold beauty of the day simply highlighted my grief. The preacher on the radio began to talk about Valentins Day. I turned him off.

FEBRUARY 21ST

The central heating boiler has been disconnected – too old to be safe anymore. It will have to be replaced, but meantime I am without proper heating – in the coldest spell of weather for quite a while.

I'm so glad you aren't having to suffer this deprivation. That's one thing to be thankful for. But you know how badly I react to the cold weather, and I'm afraid this blow has hit me very hard. Following on my difficult, weepy week-end, it seemed like the final straw when the gas man made his pronouncement. I'm devastated by the effect this has had on me. I feel desolate, insecure, isolated – in a way I haven't done since you died.

M. said a perceptive thing. Warmth represents closeness, he said. Cold brings distance. He added: 'We'll have to come round and hug you warm again!'

But there's only one pair of arms that could bring me the comfort I need, and I shall never feel the precious warmth of those again . . .

Oh, I must stop this! What is happening to me? Is my sense of God's presence, and the feeling that you are still near, dependent on physical warmth? Mere creature comfort? If not, why do I suddenly feel so alone, beyond the reach of any comfort?

FEBRUARY 24TH

The sun is shining today, and all the snow and ice have melted. Underneath the birch trees I saw tiny yellow crocuses this morning. It cannot be a co-incidence that I read something about Spring during my early 'Quiet time':

There are depths in all of us which respond unexpectedly
Along forgotten paths . . .
Thank you for the hidden things of your creation –
Hidden in nature
Hidden in the earth and in the seed –
Hidden in me.

MARCH 1ST

I finally came through that dark valley, sweetheart. But I emerged badly shaken and still prone to sudden upsurges of tearfulness. I asked the Lord to give me back my joy, and today, there it was when I awoke, like a gift that had been laid on my pillow in the night. I am so grateful.

All the same, I think I am entering into a new phase of my grieving – as the little 'how-to' book would no doubt have told me. So my grieving process is "normal"? What comfort does that bring me? It's still a journey unique to me, and one that I have to walk alone.

I've been painting in oils again. I brought the little electric fire – (my only means of heating) – down to the kitchen, together with the box of oil paints I bought you all those years ago, took a deep breath, and began. The sight of all those tubes of colour, the linseed oil, the brushes, and the canvas that fits into the lid of the box – all these things brought back so many memories of the days when I first started to paint. I was in my teens then, just leaving school. And of course it was our mutual interest in art which drew us together in the first place. But your gift was so much greater than mine, and somehow I gave up painting after we met. It seemed right to keep to my particular field, which was writing, and to leave the artistic side of things to you.

But now, suddenly, the urge to begin again is there, and I have grasped it eagerly. It was snowing outside on the day I chose to begin. D. had to cancel her planned visit, and I faced a whole day indoors on my own, with only the electric fire for warmth. But as I began to paint, my spirits rose. I tuned in to Classic FM and was soon immersed in a different world. In fact, I had a glorious day!

I decided to paint our favourite picnic spot up on Clodgy Point. Do you remember that special rock where we used to picnic, and where the sea pinks grew in profusion, and the sea crashed against the rocks down below? We used to love watching the fountains of white sea-spray against the turquoise of the ocean . . .

I had forgotten how much sheer pleasure there is to be had in handling the paint itself – the smell of the linseed oil, the sensation of applying the paint to the grainy surface of the canvas, the joy of seeing the picture emerge from the free movement of brush-strokes. I had to work and rework parts of it, of course. The sky needed lightening, the sea given more variations of tone, the swathes of sea pinks underscored with more density in the grass. The contrasts of colour in the texture of the rocks highlighted . . .

When the picture was finished, I stood back from it and wondered what you would have said about it. But, anyway, I loved the act of creating it, and feel really excited about doing more.

MARCH 3RD

It's interesting to reflect on the part this journal plays in my life just now. When I'm actually writing in it, I feel at peace, fulfilled, in touch with you in a special way Yet I experience conflict whenever I approach the task of making an entry. Usually I'm driven to it by a longing for you – a yearning to share my thoughts with you.

This past week-end has been difficult again. Sunday is never easy, especially if I haven't invited anyone to lunch So toward evening I was struggling with tears again and was on the verge of giving in to an onslaught of gloom, when I suddenly thought: 'Tomorrow I'll write in the journal'. And immediately I was comforted. I suppose it's really like writing a letter to you. Not real communication, of course, but a very good substitute. It brings me close to you in a special way.

I try to remind myself of this each time I struggle with a 'shall I, shan't I?' conflict over sitting down to make an entry. It doesn't make any difference. I go through a similar process every time. I suppose it's because my imagination and creative instinct have to overcome stark reality each time. Anyway, I'm deeply grateful that I was led to start it in the first place, because the therapeutic value of it is clearly good.

MARCH 10TH

I've done another painting! This time I've tackled the engine houses at Bottalick. Oh, what glorious days we spent there, high up above the ocean perched on the steep hillside that leads down sharply to the cliff edge. I remember the thrill of coming on to this spot for the first time, looking down to those two ruined engine houses, built down there on the actual rocks, and silhouetted against the sea. And what a sea! Vivid aquamarine, racing and foaming on to the rocks below. And the hillside alive with colour – grey-white rocks, sea pinks again and banks of yellow gorse.

We picnicked there, and you drew all day, while I wandered the hillside with my camera, absorbing the glorious views, and breathing in the sights and sounds all around me. I wasn't painting in those days, hadn't actually thought of taking it up again. But now I can work at my canvases to my heart's content, capturing something of all that stored-up beauty. Because it's all there, just waiting to be released.

I've thought a lot about this painting matter – the fact that I stopped practising it for forty years after I met you, yet found the gift waiting for me again when I most needed its therapeutic benefits.I think you were surprised when I asked for a box of watercolours and a set of brushes for my sixtieth birthday. 'Happy painting!' you wrote on the gift tag. But I didn't touch them for a while. I had done very little watercolour work in the past, always favouring oils with their richly fluid possibilities, and their scope for broad brush strokes. Now I looked at my neat little box of watercolours and thought: 'Supposing I'm hopeless at it? Supposing any gift I had in my teens has withered and died?'

I made my first attempt one afternoon while you were out,

painting a favourite vase which happened to be reflecting strong highlights from the window in its rounded bowl. I remember clearly the delight of seeing how the pale, translucent colours washed on to the cream, grainy paper of my sketchbook. But I didn't show you my effort when you came in! I suppose I was afraid that you, with your impeccably high standard, would have difficulty hiding your reaction to my feeble effort, and that I would be discouraged.

I needed that special therapy in those days, and you were aware of that, so you did, in fact, encourage me to persevere. We were both, at that time caught up in the trauma of L's ongoing condition, and painting became a lifeline – just as working in oils has become for me now. I thank God that He led me back to the world of beauty and creativity through painting – a world I had longed to re-visit, yet had held back from doing so for all those years.

When the black clouds came, I would get out my watercolours and draw whatever was to hand – a delphinium in the garden, a tree seen from my bedroom window, or, whenever we were in Cornwall, the ever-changing sea as it pounded the beach just below our balcony. I never ceased to be amazed at the 'completeness' of this activity. The feel of the summer air on my skin, the sound of the birds, or the sea, or the voices of children at play– all these things combined to make a sensual world in which I was completely absorbed; in which I felt myself to be bathed in the richness of nature's bounty. And I became aware of a deep lifting of my heart to God in praise and thanksgiving for the wonders of creation. And in this I experienced healing of mind and body.

Painting is a way of seeing, we are told. And I understand now how your whole life has been an experience of 'seeing', and in seeing of being enriched beyond measure . . .

With this in mind, I have a plan now, which excites me. I have been looking through all your folios and sketchbooks, and I realize just how much treasure is shut away, and may never be appreciated by others if I don't do something about it! I have made enquiries at our local theatre, where I know that art exhibitions are regularly held, and I plan to put on a retrospective show of your work as soon as I have put in all the necessary work!

I am really excited about this!

MARCH 10TH

I'm planning a trip to Dorset, and I'm really looking forward to it. I'll be looking up various friends and visiting some of the places we loved during our time of ministry there. This chance of a break has come at exactly the right time, because the central heating boiler is at last to be replaced, and it will happen while I am away!

MARCH 15TH

Just as I anticipated – the trip to Dorset has been a real tonic to me. Talking with friends, feeling the love and genuine interest, looking into their sweetly familiar faces, as we shared our experiences of sorrow and joy . . .

Specially precious was a day spent with J. and a journey into the Purbecks. To visit the place where C. is buried. The two of us stood and gave thanks for the memory of C.'s last days, when you were able to be at his bedside, and to hear him say that he had come to faith in Christ during his illness. So much prayer had gone up for C., and when, eventually, the funeral service had been arranged, you were asked to go back to Dorset to conduct it.

So although I couldn't be there at the time of the funeral – needing to stay at home and do battle with our own tragic circumstances – yet I stood there now with J., on that misty hill above the sea, and gave thanks.

Travelling home yesterday on the train, a woman of about my own age left her seat to come and sit opposite me. She wanted to talk. She was a Catholic, she said, had been to visit her daughter in

Coventry, and was returning with an aching heart. We soon found we had a lot of common ground, and much that we could share. I was able to underline our deep human need to forgive and be forgiven, and before we parted we promised to pray for one another.

So although I made that trip alone, yet I felt the presence of God went with me in a special way. And your sweet presence too . . .

And then to return to a beautiful warm flat! After nearly four weeks of struggling to keep warm, it was so good to hand over the keys and leave the men to get on with it. When I got home I just went round all the rooms saying 'Thank you, Lord! Thank you for everything!!'

MARCH 20TH

Someone called me 'strong' again the other day. If only they knew how this intended accolade upsets me. Because somehow I'm afraid, I suppose, that what they really mean is "tough". If I am strong, then the nature of that strength is the kind St. Paul spoke of when he said: "When I am weak, then am I strong. For His strength is made perfect in my weakness."

How do they see me, these kindly folk? A smiling face, cheerful, positive attitude in my conversation, serene and unruffled, perhaps? I don't know. If they could see me sometimes when I have shut my door behind me, they might be surprised! When I think of all the things I have had to cope with in my life, all the pain and struggle and grief, I know full well that I have built up an inner strength through having to constantly cast myself upon God. Without faith in Him, and the belief that 'all shall be well, all manner of things shall be well' – I would have cracked up long ago.

This inner strength has grown out of adversity. But again, you are the only one who could really understand that. You alone knew the real me – the inadequate, vulnerable, self-doubting person who hides behind the smiling face.

Those words of Julian of Norwich are so beautiful. I remember sitting in Westminster Abbey during one of our London visits and gazing at the inscription on the altar cloth.

And underneath there were some lines by T. S. Eliot:

When the rose turns inward toward the flame
And the flame and the rose are one.

My heart reached out then to embrace the beauty embodied in that paradox. It reaches out again as I remember, and is comforted.

MARCH 21ST

'What about those visits to London?' people ask. 'Will you still go? You and Arthur used to enjoy them so much!'

True, but those days spent together in the beloved city – visits we had made regularly together all through our married life – seem now to be a part of me which has died with you. They have come to an end, and can never happen again. I shall grieve for them, I know. But it will all be a part of my grief for loss of you, and of our joint existence. And there will be more of this comprehensive loss to be uncovered – I know that.

I remember, long ago, when you'd been to some ministers' fraternal in Westminster, meeting up with you later at the Festival Hall. You sat down at the table opposite me, and suddenly you leaned across and took both my hands in yours. Your eyes devoured me with that all-consuming love which often took my breath away.

'All those stuffy men in their grey suits, pontificating!' you said. 'Oh, my darling I love you so much!'

Amongst strangers, you would often kiss me openly – in the street, on the train, in restaurants. I loved those impulsive displays of affection. But when we were among folk we knew, you would keep your distance. You were rarely demonstrative toward me in the company of friends. But there is a wonderful sense of privacy in the bustling, roaring activity of London streets. We loved to be enclosed together in that anonymity.

I cannot conceive that I shall ever want to walk those familiar paths through the London parks again, knowing that you will not be waiting outside our favourite restaurant to greet me at the end of the day. But the memories linger on, and can be a source of joy rather than sorrow – if I so choose.

So many other memories, too, of course, precious and private memories not to be put into words or consigned to paper. Someone once said to me: 'He worships the ground you walk on, doesn't he?' I was really startled by that. It frightened me a little, I suppose, to think that our love was so transparent. And the element of private suffering we shared only served to intensify its quality, and draw us more deeply into each other.

This never affected our love for our children. How could it when they were so much a part of it? But sometimes, when the flame of love burns too brightly, it brings pain with it . . . Unbearable pain . . .

MARCH 24TH

I've been thinking about tears again, trying to analyse the different kinds I've been experiencing of late. The involuntary ones well up from hidden depths, usually without warning, not even needing a recognisable trigger to release them. They can take me by surprise anywhere – in the street, in the bath, in the middle of a conversation. These tears spring out of a deep well of loneliness and loss. A simple, basic longing for you. And they are physically exhausting.

Then there are the ones that come in gasping sobs, and somehow need to be controlled by deep breathing and a conscious calming of the mind through prayer. These I think of as tears of inner pain – the kind of pain one feels intermittently from a partially open wound.

The third kind are tears of self-pity, when I suddenly see myself as a widow, see my own grief as from an outsider looking on, catch a glimpse of my bereaved self as in a mirror. These tears are the easiest to wallow in, and need to be checked to a certain degree for my own good.

I've been remembering, too, how many tears you shed in your lifetime. For tears sprang readily to your eyes – especially in later years. You were so easily moved and often found it difficult to continue with a conversation once your emotions had taken control. One thing is certain, I know, without a shadow of doubt, that you are not shedding any tears now, and never will again. For God has already wiped away all tears from your eyes and carried you into that realm where there is no more sorrow, and no more crying.

Remembering this, my two-sided coin of sorrow and joy has flipped back to joy again!

APRIL 10TH

Easter has passed and gone now. L. and I have made our annual visit to Cambridge and are now back home again. A lot of kindly sympathy came my way before the holiday began – Easter being another inevitable 'first'. But I did not find it a deeply grieving time. On the contrary, it was a time to quietly rejoice in the certainty of the resurrection, and to see the story of Christ's victory and triumph over death in an even more vivid and personal way. I did shed a tear at the end of the Easter morning service when we sang 'Thine be the glory', but that, of course, was because of the tender memory of singing those words by your graveside: 'Lo, Jesus greets us, risen from the tomb. Lovingly He greets us, scatters fear and gloom!'

Returning home after numerous problems with our three nonagenarians, I can only give thanks once more that you never grew really old, but that you were translated to glory straight from a reasonably active and normal life. As everyone kept saying – it was a lovely way to go!

APRIL 15TH

A new 'me' seems to be emerging I wrote recently. Brave words written in a moment of rare tranquillity. The hard fact is that I can feel like several different people all in the space of one day. Sometimes. I am that maimed half-person who feels the loss of you, my beloved, with all the pain of amputation. To have had the fabric of my life interwoven with yours for two-thirds of my actual existence, so that I can barely remember what it feels like to be single – such a fusing together of two persons cannot be untangled in a matter of a few months.

I am finding that the pain of doing anything at all without you for the first time, catches me at the most unexpected corners of my daily living. The first really warm Spring day, which would normally be a cause of uplift of spirit, tore at my heart strings because you were not there to share it.

Last night a male singer on the TV burst into the room with a song about 'loving you till the breath leaves my body' – and immediately I relived the moment when the breath had left your dear body. I saw it leave. I saw the medics struggling to revive you. I knew it was too late. 'I will love you till the breath leaves your body' the Jim Reeves look-alike sang. But I will love you beyond that.

APRIL 30TH

I've been thinking again about this question of discovering a new sense of purpose, and why it is that the recently bereaved suffer such a sense of identity crisis. 'Who is the real me?' they ask themselves. Dare I reclaim some of my gladly surrendered ground without fear of inflicting on myself feelings of duplicity and confusion? Without inviting a sense of guilty disloyalty? These are some of the issues I am having to work through just now.

But even as I write this down I feel a sense of liberation, knowing that I do not have to explain myself to you now in any way. For you know. And in that immortal knowing there is no possibility of pain or bewilderment. For it is an unclouded knowing.

How does the 'Togetherness' quote go? 'I am I and you are you . . . Whatever we were to each other, that we still are.' Yes, but you are you in a different and perfected way now. I am I in a different way, too. Not yet perfected, but becoming more real to myself each day. And there lies the paradox. For while the new me emerges slowly and painfully from the chrysalis of the old, I am still a part of you, and you of me. For whatever we were to each other, that we are still.

MAY 14TH

The anniversary of Frankie's death, bringing with it all the old memories of that day. Our pain, coupled with the sense of relief that she was now free from hers. Our anxiety about L., who had become so unapproachable of late. The way she seemed to resist our attempts to draw her into the situation. Twelve is such a difficult age. Were we wise to accept N. and C.'s offer to take her home with them until after the funeral? L. herself seemed incapable of letting us know how she felt about this. Her attitude – though later we came to understand it – only added more pain to an almost intolerable situation.

Memories. And the dates which trigger them. This particular one will always be difficult; and perhaps we would not really have it any other way.

MAY 19TH

Here we are, L. and I, back in St. Ives for a week's holiday. I have looked forward to this visit with mixed feelings, because, of course it is another 'first'. Sometimes I longed to be here, close by the rolling Atlantic, soothed and exhilarated by the rhythmic sound of the tides. But also, I have been afraid that the memories would overwhelm me, that the longing for you would be too much to bear in this place that you loved so much. However, as soon as we arrived I knew it would be all right.

From the moment we set foot in this cosy flat, with its balcony looking straight down to the beach, and the green waves gently breaking into white foam, I felt you close. Last night I had a vivid dream in which you and I were folded in a close embrace. We stood, our bodies warm against each other, our hearts beating together, enclosed in love and tranquillity. I felt the soft tweed of your jacket on my cheek, the familiar strength of your arms encircling me. It was a moment out of time, intensely human, yet deeply spiritual too.

I awoke with a sense of quiet joy.

MAY 20TH

I have come downstairs early, as you and I used to do, and Im sitting facing out to sea with my first cup of tea. Yesterday, the sky was dark and stormy at this time, and the waves were green and high, crashing on to the beach below with brilliant white foam. I to tried paint those magnificent luminous breakers with the background of the glowering sky – 'wet-into-wet' – as the painters say. A poor effort, I think.

Today, the sky is clear blue with soft apricot coloured clouds reflecting the morning sun. The little chapel of St. Nicholas glows radiantly on the end of the Island, looking, I suppose, much the same as it has looked for hundreds of years. In my heart, I share it all with you, as we always did. It no longer matters that I do not hear your gentle voice responding to my pleasure with your own. I know the kind of things you would say. To me, it is as though you were actually here.

I have felt that often over the past six months – this sense of feeling you near, responding to my silent comments with your silent understanding. A kind of soul-communion. And I have thanked God from the bottom of my heart that I can never lose you.

MAY 22ND

Sitting in the harbour with L. this morning, I struggled a bit with the memory of your red sweater approaching from the direction of Smeaton's pier. You would have been sitting on the Island drawing rocks. Your sketchbooks are full of them. 'I'm fascinated by . . .' was one of your favourite sayings. Whether it was rocks, or tree roots, or pebbles on the beach, or the abstracts shapes made by the receding tide in the sand – everything seemed to draw you into itself. You looked deep into the shape and form and meaning of things, and were often totally absorbed in your inner world of 'seeing'.

When we get home, I intend to start going through the folios and sketchbooks with a view to putting on the promised exhibition. I have already booked it in at the Hexagon for the beginning of next year. Which means that I can spend the rest of this year getting it ready. There's a lot of work to be done, I know, because you had hardly anything framed or mounted properly. But I shall set about the task with joy, because I shall be doing it for you.

MAY 23RD

What a tonic it is to draw back the curtains each morning to this wide green sea! The waves are not so high as they were on Sunday, but the brilliant white lacing of foam as it breaks and spread into swirling patterns in the sand below is as beautiful as ever. I picture you sitting up in bed beside me like an excited child with your notebook in your hand. You had been making a list of adjectives to describe the sea – all beginning with the letter R – Rollicking, Raging, Roaring, Rampaging, Racing etc. 'Can you think of any more?' You ask me . . . . There is something very childlike about you at these times, and that is something most people found so endearing.

I've been reading two books from the local library, one of which I borrowed when we were here in October. This was Catherine Cookson's *Personal Anthology*, and I remember how some of her poems had moved me so much then. Now I am taking a second look at it 'To most people', she says, 'love conjures up a vision of happiness, but to me love holds all the pains of life, with happiness merely the thread that links them together'.

Because I believe this so keenly, and I know that you did, too, I am allowing myself the pain of reading these poems again. Although they are intensely moving, they are also deeply comforting.

Don't leave me in the dark existence of my being
For I am but a reflection of despair
When you are not there . . .
Don't take the spark that ignites
Don't leave me desolate of your light.
For how could I see through the days ahead
Without your presence near me . . .
Who would, of their own free will
Choose such love?

The tears stream down my face as I copy out these words into my notebook. She continues:

'I have relations, I have friends, I have thousands of friendly acquaintances; there are people that I like and people I dislike; but standing apart, there is only him'. . .

There is another poem, written on their 36th wedding anniversary, and which could have been written by me. Except that I would have had to replace the 36 with 44 . . .

This is a day filled with time;
Not ordinary minutes, clock ticking, spaced,
But 36 years of time
Packed with struggle, love,
And tragedy faced, back to back,

Barricading each other
Against the bombardment of life;
Our defences, arrow-pierced,
Not infrequently with joy,
And shared thought that makes us one in all but body;
This day of 36 years
Not free from strife
But not one of which I would bury;
This is a day filled
With all time
And endless life.'

MAY 24TH

The other book I have been reading is one by May Saarton, and is called *The House by the Sea*. In it she says some interesting things about solitude and loneliness.

'Loneliness for me' she says, 'is associated with love relationships we are lonely when there is not perfect communion. In solitude one can achieve a good relationship with oneself'

I thought of those times when you retreated so far into yourself that our 'perfect communion' was broken. Times when I longed to talk certain things over, and you could not meet my need. I remember, once, crying out silently in my heart: 'I'm so lonely!'. Yet you seemed unaware, at those times of the pain in me.

'The price of being oneself is so high' says May Saarton, 'that very few people can afford it. Most people swallow the unacceptable because it makes life easier . . .'

This process of rediscovering myself is an interesting one. And you, my darling, in the rarefied atmosphere of heaven, may well be as interested in it as I am. For you will already have rediscovered your true self.

'For then we shall know even as we are known' . . .

MAY 25TH

It's good, I suppose to let mixed memories drift in, but they can be disturbing. Yesterday L. was in a melancholy mood, and May Sarton's book has highlighted for me some of the pain associated with melancholy people. You two were alike in many ways – difficult to reach when you had slipped into that inner shadowlands. And that can be hard for any would-be companion. Apparently there is a theory among some psychiatrists that melancholics have 'closed-in' energy fields and can be a real drain on anyone who needs to spend time with them . . . Though they are totally unaware of it, they exercise an 'energy pull' on other people, sometimes leaving them exhausted and feeling compelled to get away on their own. I have certainly felt like this more times than I care to remember. But this fact has in no way affected my deep love for both of you!

You were most certainly a 'solitary', in spite of your deep need for me, and for my love, which you never tried to hide. But you also had a rich inner life which functioned alongside the occasional melancholia. You could, and did experience deep, childlike joy as well as dark anguish of spirit.

I have often thought that all those dear folk who think they knew you so well only ever saw one side of your complex personality For you rarely displayed any other than the one you knew to be widely acceptable. You had no close personal friends, but hundreds who would rightly claim to be your friends. When these people say – as they often do now: 'I loved him!'. I sometimes want to reply: "Thank you – it's kind of you to say that, and I know you mean it. But I am the only person with a right to make that claim, because I alone was in a position to love him in the fullest, richest sense of the word. For my love was the only one which contained those twin elements of pain and joy.

MAY 26TH

I suppose the complexity of your personality is best expressed in your paintings. I've been sorting some of them out, all ready for the forthcoming exhibition, and the variety of mood expressed in them is so interesting! I have decided to call the exhibition 'Celebration', because that is what I intend it to be – a celebration of your life and work. I think I shall divide the paintings and drawings into 'decades', beginning with the ones you did during the war years, and working through to the present day. The wartime paintings express so much of the trauma of those days – the barrage balloons over the Mersey, painted while you were fire-watching; the images of death and deprivation which you expressed in various ways, as well as the occasional landscape which you did in watercolour while you were stationed in Derbyshire. There are other watercolours, too, delicate works which you did while you were at home on leave in Essex. You had an artist friend, then, who encouraged you to go out sketching with him, and taught you much about painting that was to stay with you for the rest of your life. You often spoke nostalgically about those days!

The next phase of your painting career features abstract works you did in the late forties and fifties. These are bright, colourful paintings, several of which were accepted by London galleries. I know just how much satisfaction these pictures gave you. And each decade which followed had its own special appeal. The sixties and seventies produced mostly sketches and watercolours which you did on holiday; because by then you were fully employed in the ministry. But looking at them all, and sorting them into decades, I am excited by the range of subject matter, and the variety of styles. There are cartoons and character studies; comic cats and delicate seascapes; detailed drawings of tree roots – some with grotesque faces superimposed in them; there is a graphic drawing of a train crash, with the image of a cross reaching out from the sky above; and innumerable paintings of boats and rocks . . .

As I set about buying mounts and frames for all the ones which are still in sketchbooks or folios, I shall rise to the challenge of presenting them in an exhibition which will portray your gifted, but complex personality in a way that will be both moving and inspiring. I can't wait to begin!

MAY 30TH

We have been down to choose the headstone for your grave today. I have decided to use the quotation from what I still think of as 'Frankie's poem' as part of the inscription: 'Not dead, but passed beyond the shadows . . .' Those simple words say so much, and seem to link the two of you to the two of us . . .

I found two little Bibles recently – one red, the other one white. The white one you gave me on our seventh wedding anniversary. And the inscription reads: 'To my darling for seven years of perfect happiness.' The red one, of course, we gave to Frankie on her tenth birthday, six months before she died. You kept that little red Bible among your precious things, recalling how we had placed it on her coffin, opened at her favourite passage – the 23rd Psalm.

I put the two little Bibles together among my treasures.

MAY 31ST

Two or three hours before you died, I saw you in your den, sitting at the table, turning the pages of one of your many sketchbooks. It is something you did so often, that it is one of the remaining memories I have of you. Today I came across a quotation from the artist Delacroix in one of your favourite books: 'It is one of the great misfortunes of human existence that one can never be fully known and felt. This is life's supreme affliction.'

I sometimes felt you were driven by an inner need – a search for meaning which could never be satisfied this side of heaven. That need is fully satisfied now – beyond all my imaginings! But I knew you could never have survived this earthly life without my love. And I gladly gave myself to fulfil that initial calling: to carry you with my love as a mother carries a child.

And now I give you back to the God who gave me that commission.

My arms are empty, but my heart is full of you.

JUNE 1ST

I have awaked this morning with a wonderful sense of joyful tranquillity that's hard to express in words. Because you are a part of it, although you are no longer here. As I walk in the garden and breathe in the heady perfume of lilac and honeysuckle, feasting my eyes on all the rich shades of green in the newly unfurled foliage, I feel a kind of completeness. It's a sense of unity and self-awareness that is in itself paradoxical. Because encapsulated in my growing awareness of a fully rounded individuality is an awareness of you; of the reality of you; the perfected you!

Words from the Song of Solomon drift into my mind:.

My beloved speaks and says to me:
Arise my loved one, and come away.
For lo the winter is past;
The rain is over and gone.
The flowers appear on the earth;
The time of the singing of birds has come!

PART THREE

FEAR NO EVIL

It was a bright summer morning, and I was looking forward to visiting my sister in her new home. There were a few days to go before I made my journey. My bag was packed, and arrangements made with my friend Mary, the neighbour who looked after my flat while I was away. As I live in a block of apartments especially set aside for retired Christian workers, it is a pleasure to keep in touch with each other and, where necessary, share our needs.

On this particular morning I was sitting in my armchair, admiring the summer flowers on my balcony, when I suddenly felt overwhelmed with an irrational sense of fear. A cold hand seemed to clutch at my heart, and it was as if a dark shadow had fallen across my path. I had experienced similar feelings once or twice during the course of my life, but there were usually good reasons for this. Today, I could find no explanation at all for the way I felt.

As the sensation intensified, I began to panic. I prayed for peace of mind, for the touch of God's calming hand, but no relief came. I picked up my telephone and rang one of my close friends who lived two doors away. Would she please come round and pray with me, as I thought I might be having a panic attack. Sarah came round straightaway, bringing her husband, Patrick with her. Patrick began to ask me if I had ever had a panic attack before, but even as he spoke, I knew this was no textbook condition. All the same, the comfort of having my friends close by, and of feeling surrounded by their love and concern was enough. After they had prayed with me, they told me to go away and enjoy my holiday, and assured me that they would go on bearing me up in their prayers.

Elizabeth and I arrived at my sister's home a few days later, having made the journey by train as usual, and I began to feel rather embarrassed about my strange episode of irrational fear. I enjoyed being in Sylvia's beautiful new home, and looked forward to spending time in her sun-filled conservatory and garden. But as the days went by, the shadow of fear continued to fall over me at the most unexpected moments. I explained to Elizabeth how I felt, and was comforted by her sensitive, caring response. 'Mummy, what are you afraid of?' she repeatedly asked me. But I couldn't give her an answer, because I didn't know. I had been having a few digestive problems ever since my recovery from an attack of shingles the previous year. But these were only rather minor affairs, and seemed to have no connection with the way I felt now. I was determined to put my feelings to one side and get on with enjoying meeting up with friends and family in the Cambridge area.

It was only several months later, when my digestive problems became worse, and I actually had difficulty with my swallowing, that I made an appointment to see my doctor. He prescribed some antacid tablets, said I might have a slight hiatus hernia, and told me to come back if the problem persisted. After several visits and no improvement in my condition, I was advised to have an endoscopy at the Royal Berks Hospital.

'I'm pretty confident that there's nothing seriously wrong', said my doctor, 'but it's always best to make sure.'

It so happened that I was booked to speak at a gathering of ladies from several churches in the near future. I decided to take as my subject 'The peace of God' – partly because I was in a state of mild panic about the hospital appointment and was feeling deeply ashamed that I was finding it hard to claim God's peace for myself! On the morning of the meeting I sat in my armchair struggling to conquer my double-edged sense of fear. Although I had been speaking publicly for most of my adult life, on this occasion my nervousness was made worse by my uncertain state of health. I pleaded with God to give me His peace, and to make me a blessing to others at the same time!

Suddenly my telephone rang. When I picked up the receiver, I was surprised to hear the voice of someone who had been a young man in the very first church Arthur and I had served in, many years ago. John was a sheep farmer in Sussex who sometimes rang me at Christmas or New Year, but never at any other time. This was early October.

'Don't worry!' he greeted me cheerily. 'It isn't Christmas! It's just that I was having a time of prayer this morning before going out to see to the sheep, when suddenly I felt that I ought to ring you. Are you all right?'

I told John how I had been sitting, that very moment, planning to speak to a group of ladies about the peace of God, and struggling at the same time to claim that peace for myself. When I had told him the whole story, we were both convinced that the Lord had prompted John to get in touch with me just when I needed his help and his prayers. We marvelled together about the wonderful love of God, and the way in which He meets our needs, so often through the love and concern of others.

I went off to my meeting feeling strengthened and emboldened, and began my talk by sharing what had happened that morning. The women were encouraged by the fact that I, too, had been struggling to find peace, as they so often were. And when I told them of my fears about the hospital procedure, many of them told me that they had been through the same thing at some time in their lives, and the results had been negative. I went away feeling so grateful to God for meeting my need that afternoon.

In actual fact there now lay at the root of my anxiety the fear that my problem might be cancer. My doctor knew about this fear, and tried to reassure me, reminding me that this is why he was recommending the hospital tests. He wanted to set my mind at rest, still convinced that there was some really minor explanation for my swallowing difficulty. This, in any case, seemed to be improving, and he told me how well I looked.

But when the date for my appointment came through, I was astonished to see that there was a three-month waiting list! At least I could put it out of my mind until after Christmas, and I set off for Cambridge again with Elizabeth, feeling in a more positive frame of mind. My appointment was set for the end of January.

VALLEY OF SHADOWS

I had had very little to do with hospitals for the whole of my life, having enjoyed remarkably good health. But I was now plunged into an area of experience which was totally unfamiliar, and totally unnerving. I chose to have the endoscopy procedure without a sedative – a big mistake! – and after it was over I sat on the bed in a state of mild shock, waiting for the doctor in charge to complete his preliminary investigation. When he did so, I knew there was something wrong. He came over to where I was sitting and told me there was a 'slight shrinkage' halfway down my oesophagus, and further tests might have to be taken.

Later, I was given a CT scan, followed by an ultra-sound. I was told to go to my GP to find out what the results were. I suppose I knew by now what would follow. My doctor told me straightaway that I had cancer.

I suppose everyone who learns that the dreaded 'C' word has at last caught up with them, reacts in much the same way. In a flash, the whole of one's life seems to pass before one's eyes, and the shadow of death falls threateningly across one's path. I sat there for a moment with my hands over my eyes. I think I said: "Oh, no!!" My doctor stood in the middle of the room, reminding me that I had actually been feeling better last time he saw me, and that he remembered telling me how well I looked. He had seen no need for urgency regarding the endoscopy test.

It suddenly occurred to me that I should be using this opportunity for Christian witness, not sitting there looking defeated and despairing! So I sat up straight and said:

'I just want to say that I have a strong faith, which I believe will carry me through this!'

My doctor's face lit up immediately. 'I'm a Christian too!' he announced. 'So now I can say to you what I truly believe. We are in God's hands!'

I left the surgery in a daze. I had been given the news that I was suffering from a serious physical condition, but at the same time I had discovered that my doctor was a brother in Christ. Now I felt I had my most difficult task to perform: I had to tell Elizabeth what the result of my scan had shown. But first I wanted to share my news with a friend, and I called in at Sarah's house on the way home. I think she knew as soon as she saw me what I had to say to her, and before long I was sitting in the comfort of her encircling arm while she prayed with me, committing me and Elizabeth into God's loving care.

Back in my own home, I decided to wait until evening before I rang Elizabeth. In any case, I needed to come to terms with my situation on my own. I walked around my flat aimlessly for a while, but everything I looked at seemed to represent the person that I was, the life that I had lived, the traumas I had passed through. Arthur's photograph smiled up at me from my bedroom desk; Frankie's story was there on the bookshelf, along with the various other books I had written; the portrait I had painted of Elizabeth just before one of her serious breakdowns was there on the wall of my little studio. And all the paintings I had done since Arthur died seemed to glow with a special light. The whole flat seemed to be alive with a strange emphasis of who I was. This was my life . . . but what now? Was it all to come to an end?'

On a more practical level, how was I going to get through the afternoon on my own. Yet I needed to be on my own, to come to terms with what the morning had revealed. On my desk was a set of page proofs which had recently arrived, and which were waiting for me to work on them. They were the first print-out of a book I had been editing for the past eighteen months, and which needed to be returned as soon as possible to the publishing office. Doggedly, I decided to sit down and work my way through them, concentrating all I had on that one essential task. When the work was finished, I decided it was time to ring my daughter and my sister with my news. Inevitably, they were both stunned.

'We are going to work our way through this together', I said to Elizabeth. 'We don't know what the future holds, but we know that God does. That means we don't have to walk this journey on our own.'

I thought of all the times over the years when I had wondered how Arthur and Elizabeth would cope if anything should happen to me. It was my worst fear at a time when both of them were so dependaet on me for everything. But now that the thing I dreaded had actually crossed my threshold, I knew, without a shadow of doubt, that God was there in the midst of my situation, and that He would meet every need.

Elizabeth told me later that when I phoned her she had burst into tears, but then she, too, had been reminded that God was in control. The newfound faith which had come with her emotional healing was already at work in her. Throughout the months that followed – which involved two courses of chemotherapy, followed by a major operation for the removal of my oesophagus – my daughter was a tower of strength, caring for me later through the difficult recovery period. Her caring nature and her nursing experience were of invaluable help and comfort to me

It took me quite a while to understand exactly what the operation was to involve. I was originally told that no chemotherapy would be involved, but later this was changed. I dreaded the side effects of this, but did quite well on the whole, losing only about half of my hair, and weathering the other side-effects with a minimum of discomfort. This treatment involved two week-long stays in hospital, and it was during this time that I learned many lessons which would otherwise not have been part of my experience.

It was a very enlightening thing to spend time in a cancer ward, and to begin with I found the constant conversations about treatment, the making of wills, and the varying problems faced by people with young families depressing and difficult to cope with. I had so many loving friends who visited me, and I felt myself to be cocooned in love and support. But I came away from that ward feeling humbled by the way the human spirit seemed to rise above tragic circumstances, even when folk had no particular faith to draw on. Speaking with one man whose wife had been given eighteen months to live, but who was still coming back into hospital for treatment three years later, I asked him how he coped with his situation. He looked at me for a moment, then he answered:

'There are compensations' . . . And he went on to tell me about things he and his wife had learned, and the experiences they had had which might not otherwise have come about. Their two adult children had given up their fulltime jobs in order to care for their mother. Determined to make the most of the time left for them, Alan and Christine had planned outings and visits to friends which they would not normally have found time for. Their own relationship had clearly been deepened by the pressures of the past few years, and there was no bitterness, no questioning, and no self pity.

As Alan chatted with me, his wife, joining in the conversation at that moment on her way back from the bathroom told me that they had decided to 'give something back', and they were currently taking handicapped children to the swimming baths early on Sunday mornings as their way of showing gratitude for all that had been done for them.

There is no doubt in my mind that tragedy and trauma of every kind bring out the best in us all. Maybe we do not see it at the time, but later we realize that we have been enriched, not diminished, by what we have been through. We have needed to reach deeply inside ourselves for inner resources we may not have known we had.

And for the Christian this is a doubly enriching process, for the consciousness of God's presence, the daily sense of being loved and upheld by Him brings us into closer fellowship with Him. And the 'spring of joy' Fanny Crosby wrote about in her hymn holds for us an elixir of refreshment sufficient to see us through the darkest days. This was to be my experience throughout the difficult months that lay ahead.

THE DIVINE EMBRACE

When the full details of the proposed operation were spelt out to me, I realized that it was to be a far more serious procedure than I had previously thought. I was now told that the whole of the oesophagus was to be removed, and my stomach stretched up to form a new swallowing tube. This would mean a completely new structure for my digestive system. I would never again be able to eat a normal sized meal, but would need to get into the habit of having 'little and often' in order that my reduced stomach space could cope with what I ate!

The operation would be equal to heart surgery in its seriousness, and the recovery period would take several months. With the chemotherapy courses completed, I now faced a waiting period of several months before surgery could take place. Although I was given peace of mind during this period, and the continued support of my daughter and my wider family, as well as my many friends at church, the prospect of the operation filled me with dread. It was a procedure which would take between six and eight hours, which would mean being in theatre for a whole day. Although key-hole surgery was to be used, the 'invasiveness' of the operation was considerable, and there was a risk of my vocal chords being affected.

The date for the operation was actually changed three times before I was called into the hospital. During this waiting period, my thoughts went often to Arthur, and I wondered just how he would have coped with what was happening to me. At times I longed for him, and for his gentle, reassuring embrace.

One day, I looked again at the diary I had kept during the first six months after his death. When I came to the part when I had wept over the fact that his wedding ring had not been left on his finger before his burial, I looked at my own finger where that ring had eventually found its home. I had been so glad, later, that the ring was there beside my own wedding ring. But then, just before I was diagnosed with cancer, I had lost it. Picnicking with my sister by the river at Henley, I had been convinced that the ring had slipped off my finger there. I awoke next morning and found it missing.

The loss had saddened me deeply.

Now, sitting up in bed on this particular morning, thinking about that ring, and longing for Arthur, I was suddenly overwhelmed with longing and sadness. It was a bright, sunny day, and I threw back the bedclothes – just as I had done on that morning, six months ago, when I first missed the ring – and got out of bed. I stood for a moment looking out of the window, and then turned toward the door to go and get a cup of tea. As I did so, something caught my eye in the bookcase at the bottom of my bed. I saw a bright, dazzling light above the bottom row of books, and moved toward it to see what was causing it. To my amazement and joy, it was the missing ring!

Like the woman in the parable of the lost coin, I had searched the house for that ring, looking in every nook and cranny, hoping against hope that I had not left it by the river at Henley – or, worse still, slid it off into the refuse bin along with the waste material from our picnic! I realized now that I must have lost it among my bedcovers the morning after the outing, and inadvertently thrown it across the room when I got out of bed.

It is difficult to describe the feelings which flooded through me as I stood there with the precious ring once more safely positioned on my finger. Arthur was suddenly there with me. He was giving me that embrace I so much needed. He was surrounding me with his love and tenderness. My heart was full of joy, and the nagging sense of fear about the operation and my future health just melted away like the morning dew.

At the same time, this sense of being held in Arthur's embrace suddenly expanded into an even greater manifestation. Standing there in the sun-filled room, I understood that this was God's way of revealing His love to me afresh. Arthur's embrace became contained in the embrace of God Himself. It was a precious moment which I shall never forget, and prepared the way for what I was later to experience as a new awareness of the 'divine embrace'.

THE FINAL TEST

The date for surgery finally came to pass. It was a Sunday when I was admitted to the ward, and at the early church service I usually attended, the congregation were asked to pray for me. After singing my favourite hymn, 'How great Thou art', the pastor asked for special prayer that my vocal chords would not be affected by the operation. Their prayers were answered. But the recovery period which followed was more difficult than I had anticipated. I had jokingly said to friends that once I was at home they could all come and visit me – I would just be lazing on my bed looking 'pale and interesting'! Things did not quite work out like that.

The time I spent in the Royal Berks Hospital recovering from surgery taught me many lessons which will stay with me for the rest of my life. The dedication of the nursing staff, and the care given me by the team of surgeons responsible for me during and after the operation was commendable on every level. One of the surgeons in particular had such a presence of sensitivity and care beyond the call of duty, that I once had a vivid dream about him, and found myself thanking God for him with heartfelt gratitude. I awoke to find him standing at the bottom of my bed, long after I would have expected him to have gone off-duty.

There was a male nurse whose patience and devotion to the

elderly patients in his care caught my attention, too, especially as I kept getting the feeling that I had seen him somewhere before! Finally, I asked him if he had worked elsewhere in town before becoming a nurse. The mystery was solved! He had been the manager of an Artworker shop which I had frequented for several years. When I asked him how he had come to train as a nurse, he said it was something he had always wanted to do. And although the pay was much lower than in his previous job, the satisfaction he gained from the work was much greater.

Watching him escorting frail old ladies to the bathroom, or waiting outside a curtained-off bed with a toilet roll, I felt full of admiration and gratitude for such dedicated self-giving service. He moved quietly about the ward, and was at the beck and call of all the patients with never an impatient word. I felt that he showed a truly Christlike spirit.

Every morning I reached for my personal CD player as soon as I awoke and tuned in to my specially selected music. There were Mozart piano concertos, my favourite Beethoven symphonies, plus some vocal works in various styles – both classical and otherwise. My usual way to start the day was to play a worship song which had been a special help to me during the months leading up to the operation:

> Faithful one, so unchanging
> Ageless one – you're my rock of peace
> Lord of all – I depend on you –
> I call out to you, again and again!
> You are my rock in times of trouble –
> You lift me up when I fall down
> All through the storm, your love is the anchor –
> My hope is in you alone!

Those CDs were a lifeline to me during some sleepless nights, and I was so grateful for them. I was also grateful to all the friends who visited me during my stay. Other patients commented on the fact that I had a number of people praying by my bedside.

Some said that they to believed in prayer, though they did not go to church. This gave me an opportunity to share my faith with one or two of them, and to promise to pray for them, too.

The day I was discharged from the hospital was the day of the terrorist attack on some of London's transport systems. It became known as 'Seven-seven'. I sat in the rest room watching the terrifying images of destruction on the television screen. I could not help thinking that a day which was one of rejoicing for me was a day of grief and anguish for so many other people.

It was midsummer, and the flowers on my balcony were aglow with colour when I arrived home. There were flowers in every vase indoors as well, as I had been showered with tokens of love from all kinds of sources. A hundred or more get-well cards were arrayed around the room, and Elizabeth was ready to nurse me back to health again. I had been given the good news that the cancer had not spread to any other part of my body, and that it had been completely removed along with the offending oesophagus. My sister was due to arrive the next day, and I was full of praise to God for bringing me through the ordeal.

Numerous booklets and leaflets were available to help me come to terms with my new digestive system, and I thought my problems were over. I was to learn otherwise! I had lost one and a half stones since going into hospital, and my hair was continuing to fall out due to the chemotherapy. Looking in the mirror, I hardly knew myself. Having been plump since my teenage years, the new 'me' which now confronted me looked strange and unfamiliar. I had been dieting all my life, trying to acquire a better figure, and now I had reached the weight that had always seemed ideal, I was not at all sure that I wanted to be slim! But it was the process of adjusting to the new digestive system which caused me the greatest problem.

In spite of the medication which had been prescribed for nausea, I began to feel violently sick after everything I ate. Inevitably, I began to lose even more weight, and my doctor jokingly said that something must be done to prevent me from slipping down between the floorboards!! Unfortunately, I could not take the various food supplements which were available in liquid form, as they only increased the nausea. For weeks I struggled with the misery of what felt to me like a no-win situation. Loving friends and family members pressed me to eat more, and it was difficult to make them understand that it was physically impossible for me to do so.

Eventually, a dilation of the swallowing tube was suggested, as there was a likelihood that scar tissue had formed where the join had been made at the base of my throat. I set great store on this procedure transforming my quality of life, not knowing then that it would have to be repeated several times in the weeks to come. I struggled to gain the victory over despair and despondency at this time. Where was my joy? I did call out to God 'again and again' as the worship song said. But I still struggled with discouragement. There were times when the shadow of death seemed to threaten me, and I had to claim the victory over this enemy too . . .

Then one evening when I had met with a group of friends from church for our fortnightly house group, Ruth, who had undergone an operation for a brain tumour a few years previously, was asked to sing to us. As she has a gift for music, she decided to sing something which had been a great help to her during her own recovery period. She had written the song and composed the music herself, and now she stood up to sing it, accompanied by her own recorded music. It was called 'You are Held in the Divine Embrace':

In our powerlessness . . . in our weakest place –
Know that you are held
In the Divine Embrace.

From despair comes hope
And from fear comes peace that the Spirit brings.
Trust God's loving grace
In the Divine Embrace.

When you are tired and weary
Seek the Father's face.
For through Jesus' love, and the Father's grace
Know that you are held
In the Divine Embrace.

As Ruth's voice filled the room, I suddenly felt the tears coursing down my cheeks. The words were so beautiful, and fitted my need so well. And there in the presence of friends who understood my need, I felt those arms of love embracing me. Sarah prayed a beautiful prayer, and I knew she understood. I praised the Lord for His great love for me, and for the love which surrounded me on every side.

From that moment, my joy was restored to me, and although it was to be many weeks before I was able to eat enough food to keep my weight steady, yet a special healing touch had been given to me.

For I knew myself to be held in the Divine Embrace.

PART FOUR

POINTS TO PONDER

During the creation process, God counts days based on the previous nights. He doesn't say 'The morning and the evening were the first day' No, the Bible says, 'God called the evening and the morning day'. God specialises in bringing light out of darkness. You just have to get through one to get to the other.

David said, 'weeping may endure for a night, but joy comes in the morning' (Psalm 30:5). The dawn is always more bright because of the preceding darkness, just as your progress is all the more remarkable when painted against a backdrop of pain, challenge and breakthrough. Great mornings come from rough nights. Look at somebody who is having a great day, and chances are you are looking at somebody who has been through a dark night.

Since the world is continually revolving, it means that whenever the sun is shining in one hemisphere, it is dark in another. While one person is experiencing midnight, another is rejoicing because daybreak has finally arrived. So when you are having a night time experience, if you can just hold on a little longer, things will change. The same way you rotated into darkness, you will rotate out of it again. God, the night watchman, will turn your darkness into light.

The Word for Today, UCB daily readings

John Bunyan, whilst in prison, once made a flute out of the leg of his stool. When the jailer came along to stop him playing his queer flute, he slipped it back in its place in the stool, so as not to be deprived of it. The joy of the Lord is an unquenchable thing. It does not depend on circumstances, or upon place, or health, or upon our being able to do what we want to do. It is like a river. It has its source high up in the mountains, and the little happenings down in the river bed do not affect us, or destroy our joy.

Amy Carmichael

Kenneth Wilson tells how he slept in the attic of his family's four-storey house. As the youngest, he went to bed first – and it felt like a long way to the top of those stairs especially since there was no electricity up there and a gas light had to be turned on, then turned off again once he was settled. He writes: 'That room seemed to be at the end of the earth, close to unexplained noises and dark secrets. My father would try to stop windows from rattling by wedging matchsticks into the cracks, but they rattled in spite of his efforts. Sometimes he would read me a story. But inevitably the time would come when he'd turn out the light, shut the door and I'd hear his steps on the stairs growing fainter and fainter. Then all would be quiet except for the rattling windows – and my cowering imagination.

Once I remember my father asking, 'Would you rather I leave the light on and go downstairs, or turn the light out and stay with you for a while?' I chose his presence in the darkness over his absence in the light'.

Is that not what we all want most: the assurance that God is with us? David said: 'Though I walk through the valley of the shadow of death, I will fear no evil: for thou art with me...' You never have to wonder where He is, or worry that He will abandon you when the going gets tough. Whatever you are facing right now, just look up and whisper: 'Thou art with me . . .'

At 25, Lance Armstrong was the world's top-rated cyclist. Then he underwent surgery to remove a brain tumour and a cancerous testicle. Doctors gave him a 50% chance of survival. After he recovered one doctor admitted that he had only given Armstrong a three percent chance. When asked if the rigours of cancer treatment had depressed him, he said: 'No. I thought being depressed would be detrimental. But it was a very positive time in my life.'

But Armstrong wanted something more; he wanted to race again. That would not be easy. At one point he actually quit in the middle of a race, something he'd never done before. But he came back from that setback and went on to win not one, but six consecutive Tour de France races. He says: 'Without faith we are left with nothing but an overwhelming sense of hopelessness every single day and it will beat you. I did not fully see until the cancer, how we fight every day against the creeping negatives of the world, how we struggle daily against the slow lapping of cynicism. Dispiritedness and disappointment, these are the real perils of life, not some sudden illness.'

After winning the Tour de France in 1999, he said: 'If you ever get a second chance in life for something, you have got to go all the way.' That is good news. If your attitude hasn't been right in the past, you have got a second chance. Through a personal relationship with Jesus Christ you can change. When you do, a whole new world will open up to you.

The Word for Today, UCB daily readings

Our minds are always active. We analyse, reflect, daydream or dream. There is not a moment during the day or night when we are not thinking. Sometimes we wish that we could stop thinking for a while; that would save us from many worries, guilt feelings and fears. Our ability to think is our greatest gift, but it is also the source of our greatest pain. Do we have to become victims of our unceasing thoughts? No, we can convert our unceasing thinking into unceasing prayer by making our inner monologue into a continuing dialogue with our God, who is the source of all love.

Let's break out of our isolation and realise that Someone who dwells in the centre of our being wants to listen with love to all that occupies and preoccupies our minds.

Henri Nouwen

Why suffering? There comes a point when the question changes. Then we ask no longer how to avoid a particular suffering, or why it is happening to us. Instead all our resources are focussed on how we might come through it, and our ultimate question becomes, what is it for? The basic trust is that suffering, evil, and even death, do not have the last word about life.

David Ford: The Shape of Living

The first thing to realize is that God never wills suffering, but tries always to redeem it. Suffering is the dark side of the creative process, but the true artist can never stand it, and can't rest until the mess is fixed.

Susan Howach: High Flyer

One of the greatest moments of growth in prayer arrives the day I can, as it were, walk away from my feelings, discount them completely. People fret because they do not 'feel' God is close, or even that God has 'deserted them'. Spiritual writers have compared this anguish to being in a desert, nothing to the front, nothing behind, just me and God – and He totally hidden.

Being poor in spirit is being happy with this state, happy as a rational creature to surrender oneself trustingly to this hidden-ness.

Delia Smith: A Journey into God

Religion, and all its associations, can actually separate us from the spirit within if we put our trust in these things instead of using them as a gateway to the inner life of the spirit.

The first and last insight of the spiritual life is that we alone can do nothing, but that both within us and outside us, there is a power ready to come to our aid if we have but the humility to invoke it. The suffering that leads the soul to a heightened awareness of God is part of the journey of the person to the light.

Martin Israel: *Summons to Life*

It is in the valley of the shadow of death that solid, divine comforts are brought to light. But this is not all. The conflict terminates, the darkness passes away; but the spoils are permanent, and the gains are eternal.

Hudson Taylor

Tell God all that is in your heart, as one unloads one's heart, its pleasures and its pains, to a dear friend. Tell Him your troubles that He may comfort you; tell Him your longings that He may purify them; tell Him your dislikes that He may help you conquer them; talk to Him of your temptations that He may shield you from them; show Him the wounds of your soul that He may heal them.

Tell Him how self-love makes you unjust to others, how vanity tempts you to be insincere, how pride hides you from yourself and from others. If you thus pour out all your weaknesses, needs and troubles, there will be no lack of what to say. You will never exhaust the subject, for it is continually being renewed.

People who have no secrets from each other never want for subjects of conversation. They do not weigh their words for there is nothing to be held back. Neither do they seek for something to say. They talk out of the abundance of their heart. Without consideration they simply say just what they think. When they ask, they ask in faith, confident that they will be heard. Blessed are they who attain to such familiar, unreserved communication with God.

François Fenelon

We are not delivered out of the world but, being born from above, we have victory over it. And we have that victory in the same sense, and with the same unfailing certainty, that light overcame darkness.

Watchman Nee

Whatever you do not forgive, you relive. That causes you to keep striking out at others, and robs you of the joy of loving, and being loved in return. What a loss! Unforgiveness is an umbilical cord that keeps you tied to the past. When you forgive, you cut that cord. When you refuse to, you remain tethered to memories that can affect you endlessly. That is how issues pass from generation to generation. So take charge today by saying: 'This ends here and now, and it ends with me!' Learn to receive forgiveness from God, and from those who you've hurt – then offer it to those who have hurt you! When you can do that, your heart will be tender, your spirit light, your mind free, your vision clear, and your speech filled with kindness'.

UCB daily readings

Whenever I feel especially hostile to another person, or revolted by an event in the world around me, may my gaze be directed inwards to see the flaw in my own personality and to offer it to God in prayer. Only then can I be worthy of offering myself as an agent of reconciliation and healing.

Dr Martin Israel: *The Pain that Heals*

Does any human emotion run as deep as hope? Fairy tales pass on through the centuries a stubborn hope in a happy ending, a belief that, in the end, the wicked witch will die and the brave innocent children will somehow find a way of escape. In real life, a mother caught in a war zone holds her baby against her breast and whispers: 'It'll be alright!' even as the percussive blasts grow closer. Where does such hope come from? Searching for words to explain the ageless attraction of fairy tales, Tolkein said:

'Fairy tale does not deny the existence of sorrow and failure: the possibility of these is necessary to the joy of deliverance. It denies (in the face of much evidence, if you will) universal final defeat, giving a fleeting glimpse of joy – joy beyond the walls of the world, joy poignant as grief.'

The prophets encourage us with their loud insistence that the world will not end in universal final defeat, but in joy. They spoke in foreboding times to audiences filled with fear, and often their dire predictions of droughts and locust plagues and enemy sieges fuelled that fear. But always, in every one of their seventeen books, the prophets of the Old Testament got around to a word of hope. Their voices soar like songbirds, when they turn at last to describe the joy beyond the walls of the world. In that final day God will roll up the world like a carpet and weave it anew. Wolves and lambs will feed together in the same field, and a lion will graze in peace beside an ox.

One day, says Malachi, we will leap like calves released from the stall. There will be no fear then, and no pain. No infants will die, no tears fall. Among the nations, peace will flow like a river, and armies will melt their weapons into farm tools. No-one will complain about the hidden-ness of God in that day. His glory will fill the earth, and the sun will seem dim by contrast.

Philip Yancey

From time to time I am asked if my contact with so much suffering makes me doubt the existence of God. Perhaps it should, but I can only try to explain that, paradoxically, this work has given me an even deeper conviction of the existence of an all-powerful, all-loving

God who has the whole world in his hands. 'This conviction, I know, is shared by many people whose life and work brings them into immediate daily contact with suffering. True, there are flashes of anger, the moments when heart and mind cry out: 'Why, why?' What reason can there be for this monstrous pain, this anguish, this injustice? And yet, right in the midst of pain are the shafts of pure joy, the acts of generosity, of selflessness and of heroism, which reveal the face of Christ.

The growth of the spirit is perhaps the most beautiful revelation of God's love that we are privileged to see, and like all beginnings of life, it is about the emergence of something new and vulnerable in the darkness. In the presence of such mystery one can only bow down in awe

More than anything else I have learned that we are all frail people, vulnerable and wounded; it is just that some of us are more clever at concealing it than others. It is easy to forget that so much caring, so much serving is done by people who are weary, and in some ways not quite whole. Because we want our carers to be strong and invulnerable, we project on them qualities which, in fact, they do not have.

My own experience of personal suffering, and many years of working for the oppressed and dying has left me knowing less, believing more. This is my 'Credo':

I believe that God
Has the whole world
In His hands.
He is not a bystander
At the pain of the world.
He does not stand like Peter
Wringing his hands
In the shadows
But there in the dock

On the rack
High on the gallows tree.
He is in the pain of the lunatic,
The tortured,
Those who are wracked by grief.
He is in the blood that flows in the gutter.
His are the veins burned by heroin,
His the lungs choked by AIDS
His the heart broken by suffering
His the despair of the mute,
The oppressed,
The man with a gun in his hand.

He is the God of paradox.

Sheila Cassidy: Sharing the Darkness

Ultimately, faith is the only key to the universe. The final meaning of human existence, and the answers to questions on which our happiness depends cannot be reached in any other way.

If I have this divine life in me, what do accidents of pain and pleasure, hope and fear, joy and sorrow matter to me? They are not my life, and they have little to do with it. Why should I fear anything that cannot rob me of God, and why should I desire anything apart from Him?

Why should I worry about losing a bodily life that I must inevitably lose anyway, as long as I possess a spiritual life and identity that cannot be lost against my desire? Why should I go to great labour to possess satisfactions that cannot last an hour, and which bring misery after them, when I already own God in His eternity of joy? It is the easiest thing in the world to possess this life and this joy. All you have to do is to believe and love. And people waste their whole lives in an appalling labour and difficulty to get things that make real life impossible.

If we were incapable of humility, we would be incapable of joy, because humility alone can destroy the self-centredness that makes joy impossible.

Do not look for rest in any pleasure. Because you were not created for pleasure: you were created for spiritual joy. And if you do not know the difference between pleasure and spiritual joy, you have not begun to live.

Thomas Merton

As I walked, I felt the atmosphere to be incredibly pure – a warm, caressing gentleness. Joy in one's whole being. Forgotten impressions of childhood and youth came back . . . all those indescribable effects wrought by colour, shadow, sunlight, green hedges and songs of birds upon the soul. We become young again, wondering and simple, abandoning ourselves to life and nature.

Opening the heart to purity, we allow this immortal life of things to penetrate into one's soul, and to listen to the voice of God. Sensation may be a prayer, and self-abandonment an act of devotion.

Henri Amiel

I believe that God is with us, firmly rooted in the whole of creation, and in each other. Finding ways of meeting Him in simple communication, we shall find we are loved and healed, and inch by inch delivered from the grip of our fears. We just need the will to be free, the courage to take the first step and the faith to continue.

Coming to this place does not cost money. It means giving our lives, little by little.

And involves courage. This kind of service transcends every high brick wall, and every hedge and barrier. Wherever there are two or more people, grace is there. There is no dramatic claim of instant healing, but there is the continuing presence of the Spirit of Christ, which provides love, acceptance and grace. With this grace we cannot only help each other, we can face our fears together without pretence, and become what God meant us to be: loving, creative and fully alive. The choice is ours.

Grace Sheppard: *An Aspect of Fear*

From Job we can learn that much more is going on out there than we may suspect. Job felt the weight of God's absence, but a look behind the curtain reveals that in one sense God had never been more present.

Like Job, Daniel played a decisive role in the warfare between cosmic forces of good and evil, though much of the action took place beyond the range of his vision. To him, prayer may have seemed futile, and God indifferent, but a glimpse behind the curtain reveals exactly the opposite. Daniel's limited perspective, like Job's, distorted reality.

What are we to make of Daniel's angelic being who needed reinforcements, not to mention the cosmic wager of Job? Simply this: the big picture, with the whole universe as a backdrop, includes much activity that we never see. When we stubbornly cling to God in a time of hardship, or when we simply pray, more – much more – may be involved than we ever dream. It requires faith to trust that we are never abandoned, no matter how distant God may seem.

Philip Yancey

Joni Eareckson tells how immediately after the accident which left her crippled for life, she actually prayed that she would die. So intense was the suffering she passed through during those early months of recovery, that she literally lost the will to live. But as time went by Joni changed her prayer request.

'Lord', she pleaded, 'if you won't let me die, then please teach me how to live.' It was then that she started to learn the secret of the God-dependent life. She began to prove that His grace is indeed sufficient for all our needs, just as He promised.

Since then she has travelled all over the world with her wheelchair, witnessing to the power of the Holy Spirit to make a joyful, victorious life possible in the most unpromising circumstances. When someone asked her whether her faith was not actually a crutch rather then something more positive, she replied:

'Yes – it is indeed a crutch! An emotional crutch, and a spiritual crutch – but one I couldn't live without!'

She describes her disability as 'a bruising of a blessing: a terrible mercy'.

A Hindu Guru with an inherited title, and a following of 50,000 disciples tells how he married a Christian woman, and through her witness, turned from Hinduism to Christianity.

'All that I gave up', he says, 'headship of my sect, riches and land, and the adulation of thousands – nothing compares to what I have gained in knowing Jesus, my Saviour.

For in him I have riches beyond compare.'

'I am the LORD your God . . . You are precious and honoured in my sight, and because I love you . . .' (Isaiah 43:4). Write those words on your heart: You are loved by God.

SPRING OF JOY

Although most people are aware that the hymn writer, Fanny Crosby was blind when she penned most of her verses, it is not commonly understood that she lost her sight when she was only a few weeks old. In spite of this major handicap, Fanny lived a life that bore constant witness to the indwelling of the Holy Spirit.

She spent her time travelling round America, her home country, singing and speaking to appreciative audiences. One of her nieces says that her aunt was a 'sunbeam' wherever she went because of her contagious joyousness. 'This spirit of joy she scattered everywhere she went, among old and young, rich and poor . . . Her joy was infectious. People caught its spirit and gathered it into their own hearts.'

The secret of this triumphant spirit of joy is beautifully expressed in one of her own hymns:

> All the way my Saviour leads me;
> What have I to ask beside?
> Can I doubt his tender mercy
> Who through life has been my guide;
> Heavenly peace, divinest comfort
> There by faith in him to dwell
> For I know what e'er befall me,
> Jesus doeth all things well.

All the way my Saviour leads me
Cheers each winding path I tread,
Gives me grace for every trial,
Feeds me with the living bread.
Though my weary steps may falter
And my soul athirst may be,
Gushing from the Rock before me
Lo, a spring of joy I see.

FOOTNOTE

The little devotional book, *Daily Light*, has been an inspiration to many people over the years. Comprised entirely of verses of Scripture centred around a particular theme, it often seems to speak directly to an individual need.

Throughout my life, at times of crisis, when my heart has cried out for a word from the Lord, this book has provided exactly the message I needed. I have already written of the way in which, on the day after my husband's death, the selected readings were all centred on the resurrection. Similarly, at the time of Frankie's death, the whole page of texts were promises which fitted my special need.

> God shall wipe away all tears . . . there shall be no more
>   death, neither sorrow . . .
> He will swallow up death in victory, and the Lord God
>   will wipe away tears from all faces . . .
> The inhabitant shall not say, I am sick . . .
> The voice of weeping shall be no more heard . . .
> Sorrow and sighing shall flee away
> The last enemy that shall be destroyed is death. . .

On the day that Elizabeth was set free from the bondage of mental illness, the verses were especially relevant:

> I will mention the loving kindness of the LORD, and the
> praises of the LORD, according to all that he has
> bestowed on us.
> He brought me up . . . Out of a horrible pit, out of the
> miry clay, and set my feet upon a rock, and established
> my goings.
> The Son of God loved me and gave himself for me ...
> He that spared not his own Son, but delivered him up for
> us all, how shall he not with him freely give us all
> things?

Similarly, at the time that I was diagnosed with cancer, this is what I read:

> 'Be strong . . . for I am with you', saith the Lord.
> I can do all things through Christ which strengthens me.
> Strong in the Lord and in the power of his might . . .
> The joy of the Lord is your strength . . .
> If God be for us, who can be against us?

The date today, as I bring the writing of this book to completion, is April 1st. I have just settled down for a time of quiet, and have reached for my *Daily Light* as usual, And this is what I have found on the page for today:

> The fruit of the Spirit is joy. . .
> Joy in the Holy Spirit. Unspeakable and full of glory
> Sorrowful, yet always rejoicing . . .exceeding joyful in all
> our tribulation . . .
> These things have I spoken unto you that my joy might
> remain in you and that your joy might be full.
> Rejoice in the Lord always, and again I say, rejoice!

The joy of the Lord is your strength . . .
In your presence is fulness of joy; at your right hand are
     pleasures for evermore.

This seems to me to be a confirmation for the message this book conveys. My hope is that those who read it will be blessed and enriched by the personal stories it contains. For though we are all called to walk difficult pathways from time to time, even the darkest path can be lit by joy if we take God at His word. For He has promised never to leave us to walk alone.

TRUE STORIES

MIRACLES OF ANSWERED PRAYER

ISBN 978 0 86347 619 8

Sit back, relax, and be ready to be loved, inspired and encouraged by this collection of true stories of prayers answered, of yearnings realised and of healings received. Each is a revelation of God's hand at work in our daily lives, often in ways we would never have dreamed of – until they happen to us.

MIRACLES OF HEALING

ISBN 978 0 86347 604 4

During his earthly ministry Jesus Christ healed many people ordinary people – some with great faith, and some with only a little. Today, all over the world people of different backgrounds are still being healed by God. Some of the most extraordinary are gathered here.

STORIES OF COMFORT

ISBN 978 0 86347 616 7

Over fifty heart-warming and inspiring stories offering hope and comfort with their accounts of the journey from grief, sorrow and fear to peace, hope and faith. The authors of these up-lifting accounts have often been surprised by the hope that can spring - sometimes unexpectedly – from even the darkest situations.

STORIES OF FRIENDSHIP

ISBN 978 0 98347 605 1

A celebration of the joys and riches of friendship: the small acts of kindness, the laughter, the tears, the memories that only the enduring bond of friendship provides.

Enjoy the 'best of the best': a collection of true, heart-warming, inspiring and uplifting stories of friendship.